CARL STONE

RURAL RAMBLINGS

RURAL RAMBLINGS

Copyright © 2025 by Carl Stone
All rights reserved. No part of this book may be reproduced in any manner whatsoever without written permission except in the case of brief quotations embodied in critical articles and reviews.
First Printing, 2025

Compiled for my father, Carl Stone, on the celebration of his 75th birthday.
March 17, 2025

Any omissions or errors are only mine.
The effort was undertaken with love and admiration, pride and friendship.

Jennifer Milligan

CONTENTS

1 – On The Farm
1

2 – Friends & Family
57

3 – Hometown Happenings
85

4 – Humor
106

5 – Musings
144

6 – In The News
175

7 – In Memoriam
194

ON THE FARM

OLE ALLIS

January 29, 1998

Here she is, Ole Allis,
I heard you proudly say.
I stared at you in disbelief,
I never saw her look this way!

This model has no hand clutch.
It's probably just as well.
You'd only kick it forward,
so you could coast like hell!

She also has no gear shift.
That relieves a lot of fear.
When holding back a heavy load
she won't kick out of gear.

The drawbar looks a little wider
than I thought it might.
But I never saw a new one
so they might have it right.

Her paint bright and shiny,
Her muffler straight and true.
She didn't come to me this way
by the time that you were through!

The steering wheel was oddly shaped
From the time you rolled her over.
The brakes were worn (all on one side)

CARL STONE

and wouldn't hardly hold'er.

The battery box was held together
with a snarl of rusty wires,
and I don't remember this much tread
on any of her tires.

The muffler was bent and loud
But I don't think by chance.
It was the victim, I suppose,
Of some low hedgerow branch.

The fenders were all dinged
and they both loudly rattled.
That was from the many years
of tire chains they had battled.

By the time she got to me, you see,
she was quite a mess.
And what i can't blame straight on you
I'll blame on Fred, I guess.

But I was glad to take her
as she was, if had my druthers.
'Cause all the things done to her
Were done by my big brothers!

RURAL RAMBLINGS

> **I'VE BEEN A FARMER ALL MY LIFE. AS I DRIVE AROUND THE BACK HILLS WHERE I GREW UP AND WHERE I NOW STILL LIVE, I NOTICE SOME CHANGES TAKING PLACE. THE MEADOWS ARE DISAPPEARIN'.**

THE MEADOW'S DISAPPEARIN'

September 2002

The meadow's disappearin',
The fields will soon be gone.
At least that's what I'm fearin',
and it won't be too long.

For the men that scratched a livin',
up there in them hills,
well, they're getting tired of givin'
and they've bout had their fills.

See, God tilts up his earthly canvas
and with his crops, the farmer paints,
givin' us a view no less
than he gives his heavenly saints.

Those lazy rollin' hills of green,
Those fields of corn and hay,
they're not exactly what they seem,
they don't just come that way.

They're the product of the sweat and toil
of the man that works the land,
the man that plows and tills the soil,

with a weathered calloused hand.

He does his work with strength of mind
and the muscles in his arms.
Cause folks it takes a special kind
to run these hillside farms.

And it's a tough pill for him to swallow,
he's been here now so long,
but there's no young legs to follow
the path that he's laid down.

'Cause he ain't been paid near enough
and he's always understood
that times can still seem kinda tough
even when the crops are good.

He sold the cows some time ago,
Thought he'd rent out all his ground.
The hay he baled, he never sold.
Not one tenant could be found.

He no longer hooks up to his plow,
His ole baler's in the shed.
"Never worked that good anyhow,"
is what the old man said.

So, first the weeds will stake their claim
and his work will be erased.
And then the brush will do the same
'til his farmland's turned to waste

He sold a building lot, this morn,

RURAL RAMBLINGS

To a guy down from the city,
right where he'd grown his best corn,
so tall, so green, so pretty.

He wandered out into his field,
Now choked twisted weeds,
and right there he stopped and kneeled
down on them tired ole knees.

'Cause he'd spotted two small corn plants,
beneath the tangled mess.
And he should give them both a chance,
to grow to their very best.

He flung the weeds into the air
as he cleared the mess away.
And if you coulda stood right there,
you'da heard the ole man say,

"You'll be the last two corn plants
to grow here in this lot.
Now I've given you the chance,
Just show me what you got."

He smiled and turned and walked away
and headed on toward home
'Cause he knew that right there on that day
his last field of corn he'd grown.

The meadow's disappearin',
The fields will soon be gone,
At least that's what I'm fearin'
And it won't be too long.

CARL STONE

> SOMETIMES AFTER OWNING A VEHICLE FOR A NUMBER OF YEARS WE BECOME ATTACHED TO IT. EVEN THOUGH IT'S JUST NUTS AND BOLTS, WE BEGIN TO REGARD IT AS AN OLD FRIEND. ABOUT TWELVE YEARS AGO I DROVE HOME FROM THE FORD DEALERSHIP IN A BRAND NEW SHINY RED FORD PICKUP TRUCK. IT WAS MY PRIDE AND JOY. ALTHOUGH SHE'S STILL MECHANICALLY SOUND AND HIGHLY FUNCTIONAL SHE HAS LOST A GOOD DEAL OF HER EYE APPEAL, IN SOME WAYS, I SUPPOSE, A LOT LIKE HER OWNER. RECENTLY SOME OF THOSE AROUND ME, MOST NOTABLY THE KIDS, HAVE URGED ME TO SWAP HER IN. WITH THAT IN MIND I SAT DOWN AND WROTE THIS.

THE TRUCK

November 27, 2001

The ole truck sat in the driveway,
it was looking pretty sad.
The dents and dings gave away
the kinda life she'd had.

A piece was missin' from the grill,
the bumper sagged a bit.
The front gas tank wouldn't ever fill,
it had a hole in it.

The ignition didn't need a key,
a screwdriver did the trick.

RURAL RAMBLINGS

It never seemed to bother me,
I thought it worked real slick.

The red paint was pretty rusted,
The shine had left its chrome,
but she could still be trusted
to always get me home.

T'was true she'd seen a better day,
Sometimes her clutch would squawk,
but there is one thing I can say,
she'd never made me walk.

The four-wheel drive was handy
when the snow was piled high.
She'd plow through it like a dandy
and never bat an eye.

That's why I was a bit confused,
"Swap her in," my children said.
Why, she was just a little used,
the ole Ford wasn't dead.

I couldn't understand the fuss,
her looks really shouldn't matter.
Why, look at all she's done for us,
Over all the years we've had 'er.

How many times has she been filled
with fresh cut Christmas trees?
Or made the trip up on the hill,
Brought back calves with wobbly knees?

CARL STONE

How many tons and bags of seed
has she hauled across plowed ground?
And carried all the tools I'd need
and toted fence posts round?

She's brought hay bales from the lot,
the ones that missed the wagon,
And strained 'gainst loads with all she's got,
her bumper almost draggin'.

How many deer did she haul back,
when the huntin' had been good?
How many times has she been stacked
with cords of firewood?

And what about the ballgames
For my daughters and my son?
She brought us home just the same,
if we'd lost, or if we'd won.

When my daughter felt so all alone,
at her big college way up north,
a red Ford pickup brought her home.
Right then, what was it worth?

The boy drove her to school each week,
Ah, the stories she could tell...
The trouble is that trucks can't speak
Heh... its prob'ly just as well.

She totaled up a sheriff's car,
With my son behind the wheel.
Then brought him home without a scar,

it wasn't no big deal.

She helped my children move their stuff,
From hither unto yon,
And if that wasn't quite enough,
she did craft shows for their mom.

She went to school board meetin's,
to the bank and to the store.
She just always took the beatin'
and seemed to beg for more.

I guess I'll buy one that is new,
but no matter what, she stays.
I can think of nothin' else to do,
'cause my family she has raised.

I hope when people lose their shine
And they're getting close to bein' buried,
folks will look way back behind
and remember all the loads they've carried.

CARL STONE

> **IT IS A COMMON PRACTICE AT DAIRY CATTLE AUCTIONS TO ALLOW THE FARMER, THE OWNER OF THE CATTLE, TO SPEAK A FEW WORDS TO THE BUYERS BEFORE THE AUCTION STARTS. THIS IS THE STORY OF ONE SUCH AUCTION.**

DAIRY CATTLE SALE

March 2022

The farmer grasped the microphone
with a calloused trembling hand.
He stood before them all alone
upon the auction stand.

He did not have to clear his voice
to make himself be heard.
The crowd fell silent, twas their choice,
to hear his every word.

They were his cows that would be sold
in the auction ring that day.
And his story should be told
'fore the sale got underway.

He could have told of aches and pains,
of joints that wouldn't bend,
that he just couldn't stand the strain
and was glad this was the end.

He could have told about his wife,
and how she moved to town.

RURAL RAMBLINGS

She could no longer live his life
Where such hardships did abound.

These cows had robbed him of his time,
he should do something else instead.
They'd taken him for his last dime.
That's what he could have said.

The cows had always got their meal
before he ate a bite.
It was all part of the deal,
to him it just seemed right.

He might have said he needed rest,
his patience had worn thin.
He had given them his best.
It was time to pack it in.

There were stories could be told
Of cows calvin' late at night
and how he trudged out in the cold
to help them in their fight.

He could have took time to complain
'bout the ache in his right shoulder,
and of the times they'd caused him pain,
and how he was getting older.

He stared down at the sawdust floor,
Swallowed hard so's not to choke.
Could not stand silent anymore,
It was just these words he spoke.

CARL STONE

"There'll be no tricks here tonight
 you'll buy just what ya see.
Take 'em home boys, treat 'em right,
Cause they been damn good to me."

RURAL RAMBLINGS

> **THERE'S AN OLE SAYIN' IN FARMIN'—"A DRY YEAR WILL SCARE YOU TO DEATH, A WET YEAR WILL STARVE YOU TO DEATH." SOME YEARS ITS AWFUL HARD TO GET MUCH DONE BETWEEN SHOWERS.**

BEATIN' THE RAIN

August 2003

I settled deep into my easy chair,
the day's work was finally done.
The smell of rain was in the air,
I smiled, "Just let it come."

Cause today we had won the race,
good dry hay was in the mow.
We'd been working at a breakneck pace,
to beat the rain somehow.

With rain clouds looming in the sky,
We'd played that age-old game,
to try and get the hay to dry
before it starts to rain.

And today, the battle we had won,
and it will sooth the muscle pain,
to know that we had got it done,
cause today, we beat the rain.

Back in springtime, when I tilled the ground
seems like it was just the same,
when plantin' time came around,

CARL STONE

I raced to beat the rain.

I know the Good Lord has his ways,
t'aint right that I complain,
but seems like I spend half my days,
just tryin' to beat the rain.

HIRED MAN

The hired man got done today,
left a note that said, "I quit."
The reasons why he didn't say,
'spect he just got tired of it.

The fact he wanted to get done,
well, I can understand.
'cause farmin' sometimes ain't much fun,
and it can wear on any man.

It's the way he left, I suppose,
we had always got along.
This morning we had laughed & joked
like there was nothin' wrong.

There was no final conversation,
where complaints he could unload.
No parting proclamation,
He just snuck off down the road.

He was paid a week in advance
plus a hundred dollar loan.
So, I suppose didn't stand a chance
when he figured he'd be goin'.

Those few dollars that he took were mine,
but let's put that aside.
It's what the poor man left behind –
he snuck off and left his pride.

CARL STONE

I think my money was well spent,
'cause he can't look me in the eye.
That pride he left here when he went
is usually tough to buy.

Another guy will come along,
and I will treat him right.
'Cause someday if he's up and gone
I'll still sleep at night.

Well, I've gotta go and run this farm,
can't sit and chat with you.
Best get my butt out to the barn,
'cause I got extra chores to do.

> **SINCE I WROTE THIS NEXT ONE, I HAVE INDEED VISITED VEGAS. I STILL FEEL, HOWEVER, THAT THE HIGH-ROLLERS OUT THERE AIN'T GOT NOTHIN' OVER THE COMMON FARMER. JUST A DIFFERENT GAME.**

GAMBLING ON THE FARM

October 2022

I ain't never been to Reno,
but I gamble every day.
Don't need to go to a casino,
to see my money slip away.

Don't put my dollars on a pony,
or bet 'gainst the dealer's hand.
But that don't mean I ain't lost money
or that I'm not a gamblin' man.

And I don't play the lotto,
A dollar at a time
'cause I go by the motto
I'll try to keep what's mine.

Oh, I've bet on a game or two
when somebody called me yellow,
but usually 'fore I was through,
I had to pay the other fellow.

And I've never been to Vegas
And laid my money down
But I've been gamblin' now for ages

CARL STONE

without ever leavin' town,

See each time I start my tractors
and go out to till the ground,
I know all the risky factors,
still I lay my money down.

I gamble when I sow the seed,
then I wager on the rain,
in hopes I'll get just what I need
to turn the crop to grain.

Then I gamble I can harvest it
before the early snows
if the weeds don't get the best of it.
What its worth, Lord only knows.

And I've raised this heifer for two years now
and soon she will give birth.
If she lives she'll finally be a cow.
Don't know what her milk is worth

Some say "he never took a chance,
He just sat and ran that dairy."
Well son, don't try to dance this dance
'Cause for you it'd be too scary.

Nope, I never rode the river boats
where they spin the roulette wheel.
But I have gambled on a field of oats,
let mother nature make the deal.

Yup, mother nature is the lady

where my luck lies, I'm believin',
'Cause she don't pull nothin' shady
and the odds are always even.

I never was one much to roam
with a trusty good luck charm.
I've mostly just stuck close to home
and done my gamblin' on the farm.

CARL STONE

> **FARMERS HAVE ALWAYS BEEN AN INDEPENDENT BUNCH. WHEN THINGS ARE TOUGH, THEY JUST WORK HARDER. SOMETIMES WHEN THEIR BACKS ARE TO THE WALL, THEY ARE FORCED TO ASK FOR HELP. IT AIN'T EASY.**

COWS ON WELFARE

March 2003

The farmer glanced at the government sign
then walked straight on in the door.
Took his cap off, stood in line,
stared at the tiles down on the floor.

He'd heard about it at the bank,
the feds were givin' money away.
I suppose that he had them to thank
for his bein' here today.

The bank, well, he'd gone down there,
to get a loan financed,
and they said he had to come down here
if he was gonna have a chance.

See, he gets the same price for his milk
that he got thirty years ago.
And now he's here to ask for help
though he didn't want to go.

He never dreamed it'd come to this.
He'd worked hard year after year.

RURAL RAMBLINGS

The whole idea made him pissed.
What was he doin' here?

So, he stood there starin' at the floor,
when the woman called his name.
She knew what he had come there for
but she asked him just the same.

"I'm here to put my cows on welfare,
so's I can keep my family off.
I suppose, ma'm, that you don't care,
but for me that's pretty tough."

"See, it means that I don't pay my way,
to my country, I'm a burden.
And somewhere good folks gotta pay
to keep my ole farm workin."

> I'VE HEARD IT SAID THAT POETRY IS MOST APPRECIATED WHEN RECITED BY ITS AUTHOR. IT'S ALSO TRUE THAT SOME POETS WERE NEVER PUBLISHED UNTIL AFTER THEIR DEATH. HUH! IN AN EFFORT TO SOLVE THAT PERPLEXING CONUNDRUM, I'M GONNA SHARE THIS WITH YOU NOW.. ...JUST IN CASE. THIS POEM IS A VAGUE OVERVIEW OF MY LIFE AS A DAIRY FARMER UP TO THIS POINT. ALTHOUGH IT IS MY OWN STORY, I CAN'T HELP BUT THINK IT'S A STORY THAT COULD BE TOLD A THOUSAND TIMES OVER ALL ACROSS RURAL AMERICA.

FAMILY FARM

January 2, 2001

I was carried through these doors
my Daddy's newborn son.
I learned to crawl here on these floors,
it was here I learned to run.

It was here I spent my childhood,
and this is where I grew.
It was here that I first understood
what it was that I must do.

It was here I brought my bride,
and so it all began,
she knew just what I held inside,
I would farm this hilltop land.

O'er years I've smelled the fresh turned earth,

as I rolled it with my plow,
and I knew how much this land was worth,
and I clung to it somehow.

I've seen the corn that grew so tall,
it reached out to the sky,
and I wondered where I'd put it all,
as harvest time grew nigh.

I've seen the pastures green in spring,
after a winter, long and cold,
and I wondered what this year will bring,
what will this summer hold?

I've witnessed crops that were so dry,
they withered in the wind.
I've stood and watched my best cow die,
masked my sorrow with a grin.

Seen new calves struggle to rise,
still damp from mother's tongue,
and marveled at what courage lies
in one that is so young.

I have seen the lilacs bloom
in the soft sunshine of May,
and I have smelled the sweet perfume,
of a field of drying hay.

I have kneeled in the dirt
to dig out a stubborn stone,
have worked until my muscles hurt
right down to the bone.

CARL STONE

I have watched the red-tailed hawk
as I was raking hay,
floating in his lofty stalk
should I uncover hidden prey.

Watched deer and turkey glean my fields
of what I've left behind.
I know sometimes they've hurt my yields,
but most time, I don't mind.

Now my machinery line is tired,
but together it is held,
with a piece of rusty wire
and a little spot of weld.

There's been blood on most the shields
from a knuckle or a shin.
But I kept 'em working in the fields
until the crops were in.

And for those who see a gentle cow
in a pasture all serene,
I'm here to tell you here and now
sometimes they're wild and mean.

Now if you're gonna fight with cattle
that outweigh ya eight to one,
well I've been there in that battle,
and it sure ain't a lot of fun.

I've been butted, I've been kicked,
wet tails slapped 'cross my face.

RURAL RAMBLINGS

I've been stomped on, I've been licked,
been dragged all o'er this place.

Then I get up, pick up my hat,
My whole body racked with pain,
and give ole boss a playful slap
and a hearty scoop of grain.

But it was all a part of work,
And sometimes work ain't fun
so I pushed onward like a jerk
until the job was done.

O'er the years were things I've sold
and things I had to buy.
The first were always at their low,
the latter all-time high.

I've strained my feeble brain, my friend,
to make a whopping profit.
But when it came down to the end,
I just made a livin' off it.

I've fought the steady fight of old
to try and make ends meet.
I've felt the sting of numbing cold,
I've born the searing heat.

I've noticed different thing of late,
Like my step's not quite so quick
And all my joints and muscles ache.
Is it time for me to quit?

CARL STONE

But there are questions I must ask,
if indeed I've had my fill.
If I don't take these jobs to task,
then tell me, please, who will?

Who will rise 'fore dawn each morn
to tackle each new day,
and who will tend the new calves born,
and who will bale the hay?

Who will brace the big barn doors
when the wind turns from the south?
And who will wander these barn floors
when I've finally had enough?

Who will rise to milk the cow
whose udder's 'bout to burst,
and who will fix the water now
when the cows cry out with thirst?

Who will fix the milkhouse drain
and who will mend the fence?
And who will fight the wind and rain
when it seems to make no sense?

Who will sow the corn rows straight,
and who will clean the barn?
And who will work at night till late
to save my father's farm?

No one, no one, I would guess.
But I will place no blame,
for who would want to face these tests,

to play this foolish game?

I was placed here on this earth
as steward of this land.
And it was used to judge my worth,
as a farmer and a man.

And should I stop tomorrow,
Which I don't 'spect I'll do,
there should be no sorrow,
For I've nothin' left to prove.

CARL STONE

COLD OLE EMPTY BARN

I sold my milk cows here today.
The last truck just left the farm,
and I'm sittin' on this bale of hay
in a cold ole empty barn.

Oh, I've had trouble getting help to stay,
I suppose I know the reason.
It's tough to do this every day,
season after season.

Last summer it was hot and dry,
I had trouble with my well.
The price of cows is pretty high,
figured it was time to sell.

It's been a darn good run, I'd say,
since nineteen forty-three
milk's been shipped here every day,
first by Dad and then by me.

Might know that I would blow it,
I'd be the one to drop the ball.
'Cause tomorrow, don't ya' know it
there'll be no milk shipped here at all.

The price of milk rests on the whim
of some fat cat money man
and it's a game that I can't win
no matter how I plan.

RURAL RAMBLINGS

And someone's gettin' rich I fear,
Now doesn't that seem funny?
I'm doin' all the work right here
and he's getting all the money.

Guess I grew tired of that game.
It ain't much fun no more.
But life here will never be the same,
that much I know for sure.

See, I'm much too young to retire,
too old to be much good.
In town, don't know if I'd be hired,
might not wanna if I could.

'Cause all these years I've bossed myself
as near as I can tell.
Takin' orders now from someone else
might not work too well.

But I figured I should get out now
'cause I don't owe a single soul
and if I milked another cow
I'd end up in the hole.

At least I didn't lose it.
Got machinery, got the land.
I'll figure out a way to use it,
I still got the upper hand.

But there should be somethin' here it seems
after milkin' cows so long.

CARL STONE

More than a bunch of wore out dreams
like some sad ole country song.

There should be somethin' more at last
when the milk cows leave the far.
More than just a stack of cash
and a cold ole empty barn.

Tomorrow mornin' I'll get up,
come downstairs like some ole fool,
and stare into my coffee cup
and wonder what to do.

'Cause I sold my milk cows here today.
The last truck just left the farm,
and I'm sittin' on this bale of hay
in a cold ole empty barn.

WINDMILLS

June 30, 2000

We started on a project
on my ole windy knob.
What sounded pretty simple
turned into quite a job.

They were gonna put some whirlygigs
on top of some big tower
and when they got 'em all wired up,
they'd make electric power.

The whole idea seemed far-fetched
to an ole farm boy like me,
but I told 'em to get started,
and I'd just wait and see.

They had to build a road up there
to haul up all their stuff.
I had a road there of my own
that wasn't good enough.

"Let's put it there," one man said,
"It's wet there," I replied.
They put it right there anyway -
Must've thought that I had lied.

About the time they started,
the clouds just opened up.
The rain it came in droplets

that would fill a coffee cup.

Now even I know dirt and water's
what it takes to make thick mud,
and it's tough to build a solid road
in the middle of a flood.

But they just kept on goin',
not a thing could make them yield,
and soon they had a gravel road
right through my ole hay field.

There was managers and engineers
and consultants of all sorts.
I guess their job was mainly
to fill out long reports.

Who they reported to and why
I s'pose I'll never know.
I guess when you're big business
that's just the way things go.

Engineers they came by car and truck,
engineers they came by plane.
Never seen so many engineers
without a single train!

Now you can't expect men like these
to think standin' on their feet.
They all become much smarter
when they can take a seat.

And since there was no offices

up there in my hay fields.
Well, I'll be damned, they brought 'em in –
they had 'em right on wheels!

They fitted them with 'lectric,
they brought in twelve phone lines.
What on earth must they be thinkin',
What in heaven's on their minds?

I guess I'll have to wait and see
just how this all turns out,
see if anyone of them
knows what he's talkin' about.

I just hope when they came on my farm
they stopped and looked around it.
I hope somehow that one of them
remembers how they found it.

From the first pass of the dozers
it became no longer funny.
I knew what I had given up
for nothin' more than money.

I never sold a bit of land.
I only signed a lease.
What I gave up was solitude.
What I sold to them was peace.

CARL STONE

CORN SEED

I finished plantin' corn today,
the seed's all in the ground.
The planters cleaned and put away,
'til next spring comes around.

Plantin' time's a lotta work
and it's a good job finally done,
but in those fields, beneath the dirt,
the real struggle's just begun.

See, inside that hard ole corn seed
is a little bitty sprout.
Just think of all the strength he'll need
to push his pale spear out.

And when he fin'lly forces his way through,
he's still beneath the ground.
It's cold and dark, what should he do?
Head up or go back down?

When the sun's soft springtime glow
warms the soil from above.
And the little sprout knows where to go
and turns upward and just shoves.

He pushes up with all his might,
don't s'pose he feels pain,
but when he pops up in the light,
sure enough it starts to rain.

RURAL RAMBLINGS

Now he's sure he'll meet his death,
'cause he smaller than the drops,
but he sucks it up and holds his breath
until the shower stops.

CARL STONE

> THE WINDMILLS WERE UP, THE CRANES AND BULL-
> DOZERS HAD GONE HOME. YET STILL THE CURIOUS
> ONLOOKERS CONTINUED TO COME BY THE CARLOAD.
> ALTHOUGH I DO UNDERSTAND THE ATTRACTION,
> THEY ARE MAJESTIC MACHINES, I FELT COMPELLED
> TO PICK ON THESE WINDMILL GAWKERS WITH A LIT-
> TLE VERSE. AFTER ALL, THE MILLS ARE JUST GOIN'
> ROUND AND ROUND.

ROUND AND ROUND

December 7, 2000

I've never seen the likes of it,
And never will again,
The way the people come and sit,
to watch the windmill spin.

Now the mills they don't jump side to side,
And they don't slide up and down,
but people come from far and wide,
to watch 'em just go round.

I've seen 'em leap forth from their car,
A camera in each hand.
Snappin' pictures near and far
as they stumble 'cross the land.

We built a gate to stop their charge,
At the bottom of the hill,
For though the windmills are quite large,
they push closer even still.

RURAL RAMBLINGS

'Neath whirlin' blades, the cows they graze,
their heads kept to the ground.
Never do they skyward gaze,
'cause they're just goin' round and round.

The deer and turkey pay no mind,
Don't even seem to care.
The geese fly by them in a line,
as if they were not there.

Now I've seen attractions in this world,
but mostly for good reason.
Like pups close to their mother curled
in the cold and snowy season.

I've seen the bees that hover,
around a sweetened flower.
Seen people run for cover,
from a noontime summer shower.

I've seen the moths that cluster,
about the ole porch light.
And I've seen the patrons gather,
round the barmaid late at night.

I've seen the youngsters rush the stage
to hear a new rock band.
And as I start to gray with age,
these things I understand.

But I've never seen the likes of it,
'spect I never will again,

the way the people come and sit,
to watch the windmills spin.

Cause no matter how I twist my neck
from down here on the ground,
I finally mutter, What the heck,
they just go round and round."

RURAL RAMBLINGS

> **FOR THOSE OF YOU THAT HAVE TRACKED A TROPHY BUCK IN THE EARLY SNOWS OF WINTER, THIS IS FOR YOU. FOR THOSE OF YOU THAT HAVE NEVER SHOULDERED A GUN IN THIS PURSUIT, THIS MAY HELP YOU UNDERSTAND THOSE OF US THAT HAVE.**

THE HUNT

November 30, 2001

Why follow the track of the deer with the rack
in the freshly fallen snow?
Where are the thrills of scaling the hills
wherever his trail should go?

When your legs are lame and your brain's the same
why so painfully do you trudge?
It can be no longer that you're pushed with hunger,
it's your ego refusing to budge.

You just won't admit it that somewhere within it
that deer is just smarter than you.
You cannot conceive, won't be forced to believe,
that this beast will make you his fool.

So, you plan and you scheme, chase after that dream
that you'll catch him when he isn't looking.
And later tonight by the campfire light
fresh venison you will be cookin'.

You circle around keeping close to the ground,
knowing soon he will lower his guard.

CARL STONE

You crawl through the snow in the wet & the cold,
never said that it wouldn't be hard.

Your muscles are tense, you've got a sixth sense
that he's layin' up there by that pine.
You're checkin' your gun, this battle is won,
when he jumps he's in your firin' line.

You make one last push through the weeds and the brush
knowing well you have conquered his mind.
Through the stillness you hear what hunters most fear,
a snort comin' up from behind.

How did he get there? Why weren't you aware?
You'd figgered he was straight ahead.
You can't help but grin, while you're trackin' him,
he's been 'round trailin' you instead.

So slowly you twist, knowing well you have missed,
Your chance to bag him today.
He's off in a dash, you just see a flash
as he gracefully bounds on his way.

Now you've learned a lesson, you shouldn't be guessin'
that you're so much smarter than him.
Yes, you've took your licks, but you've picked up some tricks
should your path ever cross his again.

The boys back at camp have all danced that dance
on a snow covered hill somewhere.
They'll rib you for a while, then just sit and smile,
wishin' only they could have been there.

RURAL RAMBLINGS

'Cause tonight you'll eat well and huge tales you will tell,
'bout the big buck that just got away.
And I have not a doubt, that's what it's about
for big memories were bagged on that day.

CARL STONE

TRACTOR ROLLOVER

I pulled my tractor on the field,
and set my plow on down.
The soil churned beneath my wheels
as the plow points pierced the ground.

On the creekbank over yonder
there was still a patch of snow.
And my mind began to wander
back some fifty years ago.

The tale involves my brother
and an Allis Chalmers WD.
There's a role played by my mother,
nothin' much to do with me.

It had happened on that steep bank,
my brother rolled that tractor over.
Ole Allis's wheels clawed the air,
though he'd done his best to hold 'er.

'Neath whirlin' wheels he'd crawled to get
the poor ole thing shut off.
'Cause that ole Allis wouldn't quit,
back then they built 'em tough.

Thank the Lord he'd been thrown free
'cause he was up here all alone.
He scrambled from his hands and knees
and took off runnin' home.

To say that he's been scared some,
would be treatin' it too kind.
'Cause then that lad began to run,
as if he'd lost his mind.

He ran three-fourths a mile or more,
like he'd lost all his senses.
'Cause time he reached the kitchen door,
some claimed he'd leaped five fences!

He stumbled to the table,
still gasping for his breath.
Tried to speak, but wasn't able,
the boy looked close to death.

Mom looked into the boy's pale face
and whirled to the pantry fast.
Took whiskey from its hidin' place,
poured a good snort in a glass.

"I know, son, you won't like the taste,
but you must drink it down.
Hurry now son, please make haste,
it'll help bring you around."

So, the young lad did as he was told,
Ma did well, most folks would say.
But there's no way that they could know
what Ma started on that day.

See, that should be the story's end,
but today we know it wasn't.
'Cause that boy went and told his friends,

his brothers, and his cousins.

And soon all across the county,
boys took tractors out on hills,
in search of the same bounty,
should they somehow take a spill.

My brother felt that wasn't wise,
though the dumber ones still fought it.
It'd be safer they soon realized,
if they just went out and bought it.

Fake IDs would prob'ly work,
but that provide quite a task,
'cause they didn't know their date of birth
when the ole shrewd barkeep asked.

Yup, some would say that one first glass
doomed that ole' boy from the start.
But Mom learned her lessons real fast
and took 'em right to heart.

'Cause later, right here on this farm,
I fell from the ole yard tree.
And it was true, I broke my arm,
I was pale as I could be!

Now, my Mom was prob'ly near a saint,
but she still had her faults,
'cause when she that I might faint,
she just gave ME smellin' salts!

Well, the plowin' was an easy chore,

and I finished in a while.
Old memories that I'd found once more,
had come 'round to bring a smile.

I s'pose that's why I love this place
on my ole hilltop hideaway,
where memories won't be erased
and they come 'most every day,

CARL STONE

JUNE RAIN

I just can't believe it rained today,
can't believe it rained again.
How will I ever get my hay,
not only how, but when?

It just seems I am so far behind,
I should be done by now.
And it weighs quite heavy on my mind,
that big empty ole haymow.

It all started back in early June,
that's when the rain first hit.
'Fore long I realized, too soon,
it wasn't gonna quit!

Now, I've seen wet spells in the past,
might last a week or two.
But this one here just lasts and lasts,
all the whole month through.

So, now July is underway
and still I see no change.
It's pretty hard to bale hay,
when every day it rains.

See, I'm not talking 'bout some spoiled golf game
or some ruined barbeque.
This hayin' thing's not quite the same,
it's something we must do.

RURAL RAMBLINGS

No, I can't believe it rained today,
can't believe it rained again.
How will I ever get my hay,
not only how, but when?

CARL STONE

WINDS OF CHANGE

September 2002

The farmlands of our New York State,
are takin' on a change.
It all has happened just of late,
And to most it still looks strange.

There is a brand-new crop here now,
like none we've ever seen.
It isn't some new breed of cow,
and it has no leaves of green.

The crop that I now speak about,
has been with us all along.
It's one we've never been without,
its presence always strong.

For years, I've always fought it,
rarely considered it a friend.
Until this fella he just bought it,
Yup, this guy, he bought my wind!

So now up from the fields of corn,
majestic towers rise,
and mammoth rotors gently turn
against the bright blue skies.

I think we will see many more
before we all are through,
but one thing that I know for sure,

it's the right thing for us to do.

It surely beats a plume of smoke,
polluting all our air.
They stand as symbols to all folk,
to show that we must care.

For years we all have learned to take
From this world placed in our hands,
but now, for all our children's sake,
We must make some long-term plans.

So, where will they finish with this thing?
I s'pose I'll never know.
I just hope that guy drops by 'fore spring,
maybe I can sell some snow!

CARL STONE

THE WEATHERMAN

I don't think I like the weatherman
and I know it's not his fault.
I s'pose he does the best he can
to sort the whole thing out.

And I know his science ain't exact,
it must be hard to do.
But this much, I know for fact,
sometimes he has no clue.

Now on those days he just don't know
and the weather has no plan,
why don't the fella just say so,
stand up there like a man?

But no, he always plays the part,
tells me just what he expects,
knowing well down in his heart,
the whole thing is just a guess.

So I go out and mow down hay,
knowin' sure that it will dry,
'cause tomorrow is a sunny day,
so says the weather guy.

Come dark I lay down for my nap,
sleep peacefully and sound,
not knowin' that my weather map
is bein' switched around!

RURAL RAMBLINGS

I awake as always just 'fore dawn,
it is then I hear the rain,
playin' that familiar song
on my bedroom windowpane.

"This can't be right,", I mumble,
"this ain't what he told me!",
and as I hear the thunder rumble,
I go ahead and switch on the T.V.

And there he is, just standin' there,
for all the world to see.
That weather guy don't even care
'bout the grief he's causin' me.

I take Gramp's shotgun from the wall
and aim it at the set.
The weather boy don't flinch at all,
just tells me "You're gettin' wet."

I slowly cock the hammers back,
this is more than I can take,
and just before I blow him flat,
he goes to commercial break.

What woulda happened, I can't guess,
if he'd stayed there on that screen.
It woulda been the biggest mess
that I have ever seen.

As I walked through the hall,
just the other day,

CARL STONE

Gramp's shotgun wasn't on the wall,
guess she hid the thing away.

RURAL RAMBLINGS

MAPLE RIDGE

Some folks still call this Flat Rock,
tho' Maple Ridge is now its name.
It don't matter much what name it's got,
it's a sweet product just the same.

Much as the ageless maple tree
'gathers sweetness from the sky,
these turbines draw their energy
from the wind that passes by.

It started here back in ninety-nine
with a simple research tower,
and a vision in some fellas mind
to use Tug Hill's wind power.

They'd done this in New York before,
but never on this scale.
This here was different, that's for sure,
like a brook trout to a whale!

There'd be hurdles they would surely face,
But they would work them through.
So, they took off at fevered pace,
they had so much to do.

Contracts with owners of the land,
There'd be eighty-five in all,
to sign each woman and each man,
that order's pretty tall.

CARL STONE

Then there's that thing with Indiana bats.
What on earth would be their fate?
So, the boys went out and showed 'em maps,
they flew back to their home state.

When they'd done all they were able,
along came somethin' really scary.
They had to sit across the table,
from Arleigh, Norm and Terry.

Four school boards and three towns,
over twelve miles end to end.
They worked each day through smiles and frowns
to finish this my friend.

From the poor guy in the muddy trench,
to the man that ran a crane,
and that husky fella with a wrench,
their importance was the same.

From the top right to the bottom,
they worked here as a team.
No one's work can be forgotten,
on completion of this dream.

Man must use what nature gives for free,
and you sure have done that here.
And you can take this pledge from me,
there's no cause for you to fear.

The sun will still come up each day
and the moon will shine at night.

RURAL RAMBLINGS

Your kids will still go out to play
and the songbirds will still take flight.

Wild turkey and the big buck deer
will still roam across this land,
and that gentle whooshing you may hear
will soon become just second hand.

See, through all the hub-bub, in the end
the wind will keep on blowin',
into daily life the turbines blend
without you even knowin'.

In our fight against pollution
and the use of fossil fuel,
this is not the sole solution,
but its right for us to do.

What you've done here is good, ya know,
and you should point to it with pride,
'cause the wind that used to be your foe,
is now workin' on your side.

O'er the years I've sold a lot of stuff,
to keep my ole farm goin'.
Why once when things were kinda tough,
I even sold the wind that's blowin.

Now, I sold that fella wind with ease,
but he won't buy my snow.
I'm thinkin' autumn maple leaves
might be the way to go.

FRIENDS & FAMILY

THE DAY YOU TOOK MY NAME

October 2000

Things were so much different then.
and yet so much the same.
If you can just remember when,
the day you took my name.

We were so young and so in love
with our whole lives to share,
joined together from above
without a single care.

This journey we would start
what e'er the future, it may hold.
For we had vowed, with but one heart,
to each other we would hold.

Somehow to me it doesn't seem
like it's been thirty years.
It's just more like a fleeting dream
full of laughter, specked with tears.

For I still want the same thing now
that I desired way back then,
that you would see your way somehow
to love me to the end.

Things were so much different then.
and yet so much the same.
If you can just remember when, the day you took my name.

CARL STONE

THE QUESTION

February 14, 1998

I was going to ask you somethin',
But now I feel so dumb,
I can't remember what it was,
my mind has just gone numb.

Maybe I should ask you
to go out and get the mail,
or take the ashes from the stove
and put them in the pail.

Or maybe I should ask you
to fetch wood up from the cellar,
or go outside and check the cows,
I thought I heard one beller.

I can't remember what it was,
it seemed to be quite urgent,
I haven't heard the washer run,
are we out of detergent?

Or maybe the question was
what will we have for dinner
or would you bake an apple pie,
now that would be a winner!

Maybe I should ask you
when you last swept the floor
or "Brr!" I think I feel a draft,

could you go check the door?

As I lay here on this couch
my mind is getting' clearer -
the answer for my troubled mind
is fin'ly drawin' nearer.

There it is, the question,
I knew it'd come in time!
Would you now my lovely bride,
be my Valentine?

CARL STONE

YOU NEVER WROTE A POEM

January 27, 1998

"You never wrote a poem,"
I heard you say today.
You never wrote a single verse
for <u>me</u> in any way.

I thought about that long and hard,
It made me wonder why,
I'd never wrote a single word
for the apple of my eye.

I couldn't write one good enough,
you might think it's corny,
or worse yet you might just think
that I was just plain horny.

As you can see, I just can't write
like ordinary folks,
'cause just as I start writing
it all turns into jokes.

I never wrote a poem about
you and me honey,
'Cause how I feel about you,
Well, there ain't nuthin' funny.

Comedy and romance are hard
for me to mix.
I might say somethin' stupid

that I'd later have to fix.

So I'll just say I love you,
I shouldn't go wrong there,
and hope you know how much
that I really, truly, care.

I never wrote a poem
that I didn't have some fun.
I'll never write one good enough
so I'll just give you this one.

CARL STONE

IT WAS A WHILE AGO THAT MY DAUGHTER CAME TO ME WITH A PROBLEM. IT SEEMED HER FOUR-YEAR-OLD SON WOULDN'T LISTEN TO HER. IMAGINE THAT! WHAT SHOULD SHE DO? I SUPPOSE I WAS TO WAVE MY MAGIC WAND OF WISDOM AND SOLVE THAT LITTLE PROBLEM ONCE AND FOR ALL. THAT WOULD BE THE SAME WAND WHICH I HAD BEEN SORELY TEMPTED TO TAN HER OWN BUTT WITH ONLY A FEW YEARS BEFORE. I TRIED TO CALM HER AND AFTER SHE LEFT, I SAT DOWN AND WROTE THIS, WHICH I GAVE TO HER A FEW HOURS LATER.

KIDS

April 2, 1998

A young woman today asked me
what it was that she should do
to make her four-year old behave,
"The way I did for you".

Her eyes were welling up with tears,
I saw she was distraught.
My feeble brain raced wildly
for a wise, revealing, thought.

And when I came up empty,
that thought, my mind won't bring it –
I thought, oh well, what the hell,
I guess I'll have to wing it.

I sprouted 'bout the many things

that I had heard and read,
I even told her of the crap
that Dr. Spock had said.

Now somewhere in this long discourse
I noticed her attention.
She suddenly was locked
on any word that I should mention.

Something I had said, had stuck a chord,
I don't know what.
She just listened so intently
Her mouth completely shut.

My mind thought back, to the years,
when she was just a kid
and how she never listened
to anything I said.

Now she's fin'ly listnin',
I got nothin' smart to say.
I can't make all her problems
just rise up and fly away.

One thing I am certain
that she must understand,
when it comes to raising kids
you do the best you can.

Give him love, give him hope,
sometimes spank his ass,
give him honor, give him pride,
watch him grow so fast.

CARL STONE

And if you want assurance
that you've done it right
you must know within your heart
you've tried with all your might.

FIRST ONE TO CALL ME DAD

She was the first child that I had
my first precious baby girl.
First one to ever call me dad,
and forever change my world.

A living, breathing little kid,
so beautiful, so young.
She would influence all I did
for many years to come.

In her playpen, at an early age
a kid's book she would unravel,
slowly turning every page,
pointing, she would babble.

I could see it right there from the start
something special that she had.
This kid was gonna be real smart,
after all I was her dad.

Older when she learned to read
she became a book fanatic.
Only child I've ever seen
play library in the attic.

She'd go up there on a rainy day,
line the books up on a shelf,
and if her siblings wouldn't play,
she'd check books out to herself.

CARL STONE

Back then she was so cute and sweet,
soon we saw another side.
Found out she had a stubborn streak
about a mile wide.

But see, that's really not all that bad,
when she puts her mind into it,
she would give it all she had
and just go out and do it.

Didn't matter, really, what it was,
she would set it in her mind.
Some small thing, or noble cause,
she'd accomplish it in time.

When she was only twelve years old
ya' know what she told me?
She already then had set her goal –
valedictorian she would be.

Then she'd continue with her schoolin'
and become an engineer.
She said that back then, no foolin'.
From that course she never veered.

Her high school years flew by so fast,
cheerleading and band.
She finished top of her whole class,
just as she had planned.

Then she took off to college,
left the rest of us back here.

RURAL RAMBLINGS

Filled her head right full of knowledge
and came home an engineer.

Education wasn't all she had
when she came home again.
She came draggin' in some Irish lad,
by the name of Milligan.

The two were married 'fore too long.
He was a lucky man to get her.
And her choice of him was never wrong,
she could not have chosen better.

Engineering jobs here and there,
had two children of their own.
Finally, they settled here,
right back close to home.

She was very good at what she did,
she climbed the corporate ladder.
But it seemed to her some things had slipped,
some things that really mattered.

Things like kids, family, and home,
not stressed by corporate greed.
A library of her very own
could fill her workplace need.

And that's how you got her here today,
this is bigger that the attic.
I guess it'd still be safe to say,
she's still a book fanatic.

CARL STONE

She has excelled in all she's tried,
everything she's ever done,
and this ole heart just swells with pride
at the woman she's become.

'Cause she was the first child that I had
my first precious baby girl.
First one to ever call me dad,
and forever change my world.

IF I COULD CHOOSE MY SON

August 18, 2012

I had myself a pair of girls,
they were my pride and joy.
I still thought I'd give it one more whirl,
see if I could get a boy.

I thought if I could only choose my son,
pick out the little tyke.
If I could pick from anyone,
just what would he be like?

He'd be a bright and handsome lad
that much I could see.
'Cause if I was gonna be his dad,
what else could he be?

The outdoors would be his favorite place,
even when he was still young.
He'd love to romp through open space,
if I could choose my son.

He'd fight with his sisters some,
'spose sometimes with his mother,
but after all is said and done,
they'd always back each other.

If he played sports, he'd be the best,
and if they should lose a game,
he'd still be better than the rest,

the coach would be to blame.

He'd throw hay all day on the farm,
even though that's not much fun.
Then help with chores down in then barn,
if I could choose my son.

I'd help him and he'd help me
'cause that's just how things are done.
That's just the kinda guy he'd be,
if I could choose my son.

From that small boy, he'd just keep growin',
while I'd be farmin' best I can.
The one day, without me knowin',
he'd become a fine young man.

I thought then if only I could pick his bride,
what a beauty she would be.
The woman who'd stand by his side
for all eternity.

Not just any girl would do the trick,
no city girl for my son.
He'd have to have a country chick
that liked to have some fun.

She'd have to learn to take our kiddin',
'cause that's just something that we do.
She'd soon learn that all our ribbin'
would just mean we love her too.

She'd also have to be real smart,

no dummy for my son.
And she'd hafta have a great big heart
if she's gonna be the one.

She might have a funny little laugh
that could only be her own.
Until the day would come at last
and she'd become a Stone.

'Cause from the moment that they'd meet, you see,
past loves would all take wing.
'Cause this was what was meant to be,
it would be the real thing.

They were all dreams from way back when.
What are the odds that they'd come true?
That I could choose my son and then
pick out his young bride too?

Can't believe I'm standin' here today
those dreams have all come true.
The only thing that I can say,
I'm so proud of both of you!

CARL STONE

IT STARTED IN TINKER HOLLOW

It started down in Tinker Hollow,
moved to the Brookfield hills.
She always knew he'd follow,
'cause she'd promised him some thrills.

The wedding joined the two as one,
they had no master plan.
Soon one-by-one the babies came
and they had themselves a clan.

The little shits were everywhere
just runnin' 'round the farm.
Nobody really seemed to care
longs they didn't come to harm.

They weren't always loving, warm,
sometimes they fought like hell,
but between them soon a bond would form
that would later serve them well.

Those kids, they kept on growin'
in both body and in mind.
They were preparing, without knowin',
what was comin' down the line.

The older ones soon left the nest
only to return.
But as they conquered each life's test
a new lesson they would learn.

RURAL RAMBLINGS

No matter if it all went wrong
they weren't out there all alone.
Whatever problem came along
they could always come back home.

Then the first big crisis hit –
their dad was forty-two
when his heard decided it would quit
and he barely made it through.

But these kids knew just what must be done
and they took it to great length.
They gathered round him, every one,
and he drew upon their strength.

Then, for a time, things rolled along
mostly like they should.
Nothin' terrible went wrong.
Their luck was runnin' good.

Then one night while on a ride
the driver drove too fast.
The car swerved and went into a slide
then came that awful crash.

A helicopter was called in,
one young man had struck his head.
They flew off in the night with him.
His life, hung by a thread.

Once more they rushed off, filled with fright
to be with him at last

and stayed to help him in his fight
until the danger passed.

Now some would say he ain't right yet.
they didn't know the boy before.
I'd say it's as good as he will get,
we can't expect much more.

Yup, they've faced house fires, car wrecks,
now and they they've had some fun,
operations, broken necks,
and they've licked 'em, one by one.

And now an illness has attacked,
that spans two generations.
And they've lined up to fight it back
without any hesitations.

They're determined that they'll beat it
one way or another
'cause they've gathered to defeat it,
mother, father, sister, brother.

Find "family" in the dictionary
and if I don't miss my hunch,
though for sure it will be kinda scary,
You'll find a picture of this bunch!

FAMILY REUNION

Wish Ole Lee and Queen could see us now —
I wonder what they'd say?
To think they started this somehow
way back there in their day.

'Cause as I gaze across this scraggly crew
some things come to mind.
To be a Stone ain't tough to do,
there are so many kinds.

Now some of us had no voice,
we were born into this clan,
but those of us that had a choice,
well, just look around you, man!

Some are plump and some are thin,
some short and some are tall.
Whatever shape a Stone comes in
doesn't matter much at all.

Some, like me, ain't all that bright.
Some, smart as a whip.
Some won't say two words all night
and some won't shut their lip.

Some of us are getting old.
Sure glad that I'm not there.
But most true Stones it should be told
still have all their hair.

CARL STONE

By the looks of all these children, dear,
we must be a fertile bunch.
Unless someone just dropped 'em here
in hopes we'd feed them lunch.

It's fitting we should honor both
our family and our nation
and proudly thank the Lord for both
on this great celebration.

When the party here finally ends
and you head back to your home,
just remember this my friends,
wherever you should roam.

You may sometimes have a lonely day
but you'll never be alone
as long as you can proudly say
"Thank God that I'm a STONE".

RURAL RAMBLINGS

MY NIECE GOT MARRIED AND I WAS ASKED IF I COULD WRITE SOMETHING POETIC FOR THE OCCASION. I WROTE THIS.

THE WEDDING

For Alicia & Josh
June 14, 2003

The old man eyed the smiling pair,
as they walked back down the aisle.
His gnarled fingers grasped the chair,
'cross his face appeared a smile.

His thoughts took him to way back when,
he, himself had made that vow,
and the things he didn't know back then,
and the things that he knew now.

The wedding's beauty soon will fade,
though beautiful it was.
It was the marriage that was made
that made it a worthy cause.

Oh, they will have their little spats,
but they really will not matter.
One should expect a bit of that
as they climb the marriage ladder.

See, the rungs will all get stronger

as they continue to climb up,
'cause the fall's a whole lot longer
as they get closer to the top.

Marriage has a benefit,
if it's one that's straight and true.
And he should let them in on it
and tell them what he knew.

That their pain will all be cut in half
when they encounter real trouble.
And with the good times that they'll have,
their joy will all be doubled.

He wished to tell them at the door,
what would happen 'fore they're done.
He just shook their hands and said no more,
'cause finding out was half the fun.

RURAL RAMBLINGS

I NEVER GOT A POEM

"I never got a poem,"
today I heard you whine,
as if I've nothing else to do,
as if I've got the time.

It takes a lot of thought
to put my feelings into verse.
It's just not something that you do,
sometimes you must rehearse.

But I will try to do it,
I'll try to do my best.
I feel like I'm in high school,
and this is a pop test.

I could talk about the many things
that you have seen and done.
I could carry on and on and on,
tell you you're number one!

Accomplishment too quickly fade,
possessions never last,
things that happened yesterday,
today are in the past.

It's who you are, I guess,
that brings me the most pride.
The woman, mother, wife,
the person that's inside.

CARL STONE

So now you've got your poem,
now you've got your rhyme,
so now at last, at long, long, last,
I won't have to hear you whine.

RURAL RAMBLINGS

DEAR NANCY

The say one loses brain cells
every single day,
and I would say what few I had,
have up and flown away!

It's the number that you start with,
makes a difference I suppose,
and I was barely cheated,
as most everybody knows!

I received your invitation,
and I figured I would go,
unless I was too deathly ill,
or there was too much snow.

Now sometimes family doin's
are just too far away.
Sometimes I am plantin' corn
Sometimes we're balin' hay.

But this one I can go to,
this time I've got a shot,
but by the time the day arrived,
I just plain forgot!

"But what about your lovely wife?",
I'm sure you must respond.
And I will take this chance to note
that she is truly blonde.

CARL STONE

So next time you see Donna,
give her my congrats,
and gently tell her how it is,
with "The Uncle That Forgets".

CRUMB WEDDING

After years of sittin' on the edge,
we've gathered here tonight,
to watch this couple take the pledge
and the whole thing just feels right.

Some might say, why do it now,
at this time that you have chose?
after all why should you buy the cow...
well, you know how it goes.

See, love has no set time frame,
no moment, wrong or right
to love each second is the same
and this is now their night.

O'er years their lasting love has grown
and brought them on their way
and tonight they will be joined as one
on this their wedding day.

May they be blessed by God above
and their lives be full and long
with everlasting burning love
just like an old love song.

I've heard it said that love is blind
and right here we have the proof
cause this sweet girl has lost her mind
if you want to know the truth.

HOMETOWN HAPPENINGS

> BACK IN THE YEAR 1891, IN A YMCA GYM, A FELLA BY THE NAME NAISMITH, HUNG A COUPLE OF PEACH BASKETS TEN FEET OFF THE FLOOR AND BASKETBALL WAS BORN. NOW, I DON'T THINK OLE JIM EVER THOUGHT IT'D TURN INTO THE MULTI-BILLION-DOLLAR BUSINESS THAT IT IS TODAY. THE GAME IN ITS PUREST FORM, AWAY FROM THE TV CAMERAS AND MILLION-DOLLAR CONTRACTS, CAN STILL BE FOUND IN SMALL COUNTRY HIGH SCHOOLS ACROSS RURAL AMERICA.

SENIOR NIGHT

March 12, 2002

Once more it was a Friday's eve
and I'd been goin' out since fall,
to local high school gyms to see
my boy play basketball.

We would travel to a little school,
no matter what its name,
'Cause I was sure, when we were through,
that we would win this game.

The gym was old and poorly lit,
but the bleachers all were packed.
And now that I look back on it,
I shoulda seen the deck was stacked.

CARL STONE

I figured we could run this show.
We had more skill and height.
The one thing that I didn't know,
it was their "senior night."

It was the night they'd honor kids,
about to play their last home game.
And no matter what they said or did,
it would never be the same.

See, their dads had played here on this floor,
right here in this same gym.
And they'd all been here times before,
in days from way back when.

They lined the seniors on the floor,
just before they played the game.
Lord, how that crowd did roar,
as they called out each kid's name.

They brought their folks down on the court,
amidst the cheers and screams, loggers, farmers, working sort,
all dressed in their best jeans.

They hugged their sons with shameless pride,
waved their old hats up to the crowd.
And I felt just what they felt inside.
My God, that crowd was loud.

Farmer's hats held over thumping chests,
the ole school song they sang.
They belted out their very best
until the rafters rang.

RURAL RAMBLINGS

Oh sure, this should be a breeze alright,
I think we've got 'em on the run.
There's no spirit here tonight,
this is gonna be some fun.

I looked to my son across the gym,
where our boys politely stood.
I saw him shake his head and grin,
I knew he understood.

Those guys would not lay down tonight,
they didn't care if we were better.
They would play with all their might
for their ole alma mater.

There were no scholarships to pay,
No big money deals at all,
just rag-tag boys that loved to play
the game of basketball.

They were here to play for Mom & Dad
and good old hometown pride,
and they would give it all they had.
They would reach down deep inside.

Now, I've watched games in the NBA,
and I've seen the final four,
but I ain't seen nobody play,
like they played on that gym floor.

There were no dunks slammed through the rim.
Nobody was that tall.

But that night, in that grand old gym,
those boys played basketball.

We didn't get our butts kicked.
Our boys, they kept it close.
But in the end, we did get licked,
'cause we were playin' all those ghosts.

So, if you wanna feel the sights and sounds
of the game played when it's right,
go to a sleepy valley town,
and go on "senior night."

RURAL RAMBLINGS

CLASS REUNION

'Twas the reunion of his class,
it had been so long ago.
Now he had finally come at last
to see his high school beau.

They were an item, way back then,
he was the high school jock.
She was the one who cheered for him.
He took her to the hop.

He ran his hands through his silver hair,
or what was left of it.
He sure hoped that she was there,
he'd make the best of it.

He searched the crowd through and through,
then she finally caught his eye.
He blinked, not knowing what to do,
his huge belly heaved a sigh.

Boy! She'd sure let herself go,
what a pity, what a shame.
Why, she'd put on twenty pounds or so,
barely looked like his ole flame.

He fumbled for his trusty cane
and pulled himself up real slow.
Well, she was the reason that he came –
might's well go and say hello.

CARL STONE

It was the right thing for him to do,
he had some time to kill.
He'd go over, say a word or two,
and give the poor girl a thrill.

When he hobbled close, he spoke her name,
she turned her face to show him,
but she must have thought that he had changed
why, she didn't even know him.

She didn't have too much to say
and she told him it'd been swell.
He muttered as she walked away
poor girl's lost her mind as well!

> THERE ARE NO DOUBT THOSE OF YOU OUT THERE ASKING YOURSELVES, " WHAT COULD POSSIBLY QUALIFY THAT OLE FARMER TO SPEAK AT SUCH AN IMPORTANT EVENT?" WELL, I THOUGHT ABOUT THAT MYSELF FOR A BIT WHEN I REALIZED THIS SIMPLE FACT. THERE HAS BEEN A CHILD WITH THE LAST NAME OF STONE IN THIS SCHOOL CONTINUOUSLY SINCE 1945. ALL DIRECT DESCENDANTS OF MY MOM AND DAD. WHILE THIS MAY OR MAY NOT BE SOME KIND OF RECORD WE SEEM TO HAVE IT COVERED FOR AT LEAST ANOTHER FIFTEEN YEARS. HOWEVER INTERESTING THAT PIECE OF TRIVIA MAY BE, THE REAL REASON THAT I'M HERE IS AN OLD FRIEND, DOUG FORD, CALLED AND ASKED ME. SO, IF YOU HAVE ANY COMPLAINTS IN REGARDS TO THE STRUCTURE OR CONTENT OF MY PRESENTATION HERE TODAY, PLEASE FEEL FREE TO CALL ANYTIME, DAY OR NIGHT, SEVEN DAYS A WEEK. DOUG'S NUMBER IS IN THE BOOK.

GOOD OLE MCS

September 23, 2003

In the little town of Madison
Back in nineteen thirty-two.
The work they'd started, finally done,
they had a brand-new school.

The people came from all around
to get a look inside.
It was the center of the town,

a source of immense pride.

So large that it cannot be filled,
the people then would say.
But those ole farmers on the hills
set out to fill it anyway.

So additions were put on it
as the years went by.
And the people looked upon it
with a prideful caring eye.

But it's a struggle for a small town
to keep up in this great race.
'Cause progress goes in leaps and bounds
at such a frightening pace.

So a merger then was talked about
with schools just down the road.
The people answered with a shout
in a resounding NO!

Sure, learning was what it's about.
But it was even more.
Like the kids that played their hearts out
right there on that gym floor.

All the hot night graduations,
all the concerts, all the plays,
all a part of education
back in their ole school days.

And what about those ole school dances,

while they listened to the band,
when some shy boy took his chances,
and tried to hold her hand.

For some it was the big events,
for others just the small,
but even if it made no sense,
that ole buildin' touched 'em all.

See, to them that school was so much more
than just concrete and lumber,
'cause it held memories for sure
too numerous to number.

It was a measure of their strength,
and of their pride I guess.
'Cause they would go to any length
to save ole MCS.

That brings us right to where we are,
at a building dedication.
What do we think we've gained thus far
with this massive renovation?

Exactly what was our main goal
when we fixed up this ole school?
The truth of it should now be told
lest some of us be fooled.

Will our kids all now be smarter?
I can't imagine so.
Will they all study harder?
The Good Lord only knows.

CARL STONE

Now will our staff achieve perfection
as they go about their tasks?
Flawless in their direction?
That would be a lot to ask.

NO, There is no guaranteed success,
Just an opportunity,
For those that come to MCS
to be the best that they can be.

This building shows the faith we have,
and we will boast of it,
in our great children and our staff
to make the most of it.

And now a tribute we should pay,
to those back in thirty-two,
for where we've been, and are today,
and what we've yet to do.

'Cause it's a building that we dedicate,
and it's fitting that we do it.
Just remember what will make it great
are the PEOPLE that pass through it.

RURAL RAMBLINGS

> **I'M A HIGH SCHOOL BASKETBALL FAN. THE MEMORIES MADE AND LESSONS LEARNED ON THOSE COURTS WILL LAST A LIFETIME.**

THE SHOT

September 2002

There are lessons to be learned
from high school basketball.
A place where memories are earned
by kids who give their all.

He leaped from his defensive stance,
stole the ball right in full stride.
At last, he's finally got his chance,
the path was clear and wide.

In practice, he had dunked the ball
so many times before,
and tonight he guessed he'd show 'em all
as above the rim he'd soar.

If he could only get his steps just right
then he'd leap and slam it home
but that was not to be tonight
as the crowd let out a groan.

For as he struggled to adjust his stride,
and he knew that was the key,
alas his dribble moved inside
and the ball bounced off his knee.

CARL STONE

Now, his efforts to retrieve that ball
ended in a belly slide,
and as he crashed into the wall,
what hurt most was just his pride.

T'was the same kid, same sport,
just a different night and time.
Same ball, same court,
and the game was on the line.

The ball just hung in the air
after it left the shooters hand.
The hometown coach sprang from his chair,
a gasp rose from the stands.

See, there were fifteen seconds on the clock,
we were ahead by one.
Just hold the ball until it stops
and this game would be won.

But, somewhere before the three-point line,
this kid just pulled the trigger.
He must have felt this was his time,
at least that's what I figure.

He wasn't gonna hold the ball
and wait for them to foul.
He just stepped up to take it all
and end it here and now.

He'd be the hero here tonight,
or the one that lost it all.

RURAL RAMBLINGS

It all depended on the flight
of one high arcing basketball.

I didn't watch the ball sail high,
to see where it would go.
I just looked into the shooter's eyes
'cause only he would know.

A clenched fist he held into the air.
A grin came 'cross his face.
I knew that when the ball got there,
it would surely find its place.

The hometown crowd let out a roar,
I still can hear it yet.
Our victory was sealed for sure
as the ball dropped through the net.

It won't go down in history.
I'm sure most folks have forgot.
Except for the likes of me,
and my son, who took the shot.

The coach just said, "nice shot kid,
not the one you shoulda took,
but I guess I'm kinda glad you did,
though it's not exactly by the book."

Sometimes in life you gotta take that shot
though it's on the foolish side,
'cause whether it goes in or not,
at least you'll know you've tried.

CARL STONE

MADISON FFA

November 2003

There's been changes in the FFA
since I was in this place.
Technology has led the way
and the FFA kept pace.

Why, the biggest change we had back then
was when they let in a girl!
Some folks thought it'd be the end
of FFA, if not the world!

Well, it seems as if we have survived,
at least as far as I can tell.
The FFA is still alive
and doing pretty well.

But as each transformation reaches us
and we undergo each change,
the things FFA teaches us
somehow remain the same.

Like leadership and honesty,
and working as a team,
service to community,
and holding fast onto one's dream.

It teaches pride in who you are
and in what you can become.
And you can't go in it very far

RURAL RAMBLINGS

'fore you find out you're havin' fun.

Much of the good that in this chapter,
well, we all know who's to blame.
We recognize his boisterous laughter,
no need for me to say his name.

Yes, there's just one thing that I can say
as I gaze across this banquet hall,
those girls in the FFA?
They didn't hurt this bunch at all.

CARL STONE

MCS - 75 YEARS

It all started back in thirty-two,
with some people and a dream,
to build for us a brand-new school,
like this town had never seen.

Built on the Cherry Valley Turnpike,
for all passers-by to view,
a grand and bold, inspiring sight,
would be this glorious school.

It would cost almost one-hundred grand,
the voters had approved it.
Now they must face the task at hand
and just go out and do it.

No computer graphics I expect
would help them with their plan,
just the vision of an architect
and a draftsman's steady hand.

No computer driven spreadsheets,
to keep the costs in line.
How could mere men perform such feats,
with just a well-trained mind?

This job would have no cell phones.
How would they ever get supplies?
Could just good planning all alone
keep this bunch organized?

RURAL RAMBLINGS

The power tools we used today
were rare, or not at all.
Muscle power ruled the day,
to build these strong brick walls.

There'd be no lasers on this job,
to keep walls straight and true.
A level and an old plumb-bob,
I guess would have to do.

So many things we can choose,
weren't invented way back then.
Why, they didn't even have to use,
a simple ball point pen.

The reasons that I point this,
is so you might view the change.
Hoping yet that you won't miss,
our goals are still the same.

To provide more than education
for every boy and girl,
but a solid preparation
for an ever-changing world.

This edifice back then, as now,
if I may speak the truth,
stands as a symbol strong and proud
of commitment to our youth.

It has withstood all adversity,
from strong gales to politics,

CARL STONE

and stands here now with dignity,
in spite of all those licks.

We honor those in thirty-two
for their courage and their vision,
and all of those 'tween then and now
who upheld this fine tradition.

So, Alumni, today 'fore you depart,
look back at your success.
Remember where you got your start
at good ole MCS.

POETRY CONTEST

'Twas a typical spring day
at good ole MCS.
The poets gathered on the stage,
to give us all their best.

Some of them were pretty short,
and some were kinda tall.
Some seemed like the nervous sort,
and some weren't scared at all.

Some wrote their sonnets with great ease,
for others it was tough,
but they gathered here today to please
their listeners with their stuff.

And now the day has finally come,
'neath their breaths they whisper lines,
much as they have already done
at least a hundred times.

Now, we'll pick a winner from this bunch,
but people don't you fear,
from what I've seen, I've got a hunch,
there are no real losers here.

'Twas a typical spring day
at good ole MCS.
The poets gathered on the stage,
to give us all their best.

CARL STONE

THE BANK

If you've never been down to my bank,
you don't know what you're missin'.
It would be worth the trip, I think,
just to watch and listen.

They've got themselves a pair of Debs,
the one she runs the show.
The other one drops by midday,
if she's got no place else to go!

They've got one there, a sweet young thing,
the one that they call Kelly.
Then there's the one that does the work,
that woman would be Ellie.

There is one left down on the end
and that would be Diane.
I'm not sure how she fits in
to anybody's plan.

'Cause what she really does,
well, it's hard to explain.
I guess her job is mostly
just to entertain.

So next time you're in Waterville
or maybe passin' through
and if you've got some time to kill,
stop on in, check out their crew.

HUMOR

CARL STONE

> SOME THINGS ARE LIKE THAT FAUCET DRIPPING IN THE SINK. YOU CAN HEAR IT; IT ISN'T ALL THAT ANNOYING. AND MAYBE IF YOU DO NOTHING, IT WILL STOP. BUT IT WON'T. SUCH WAS THE CASE OF MY WIFE WANTING TO LEARN TO DRIVE A MOTORCYCLE. SO, WITH SOME TREPIDATION I SET OUT TO FIX IT.

THE HONDA

August 18, 2003

My wife told me it would be fun,
if she could drive a motorcycle.
My first impulse was to turn and run,
just pretend that I'd gone psycho.

'Cause I'd seen this woman drive a car,
watched her run the ole lawn mower.
But this was different by far,
she best take this a little slower.

So, I calmly told her how it was –
it ain't as easy as it seems.
She said she only asked because,
it was just one of her dreams.

Stubborn, was not the word I said,
Though strong-willed would prob'ly fit.
'Cause when she gets somethin' in her head,
most times she just won't quit.

She went out and got her bike permit,

said she guessed she'd take a ride.
I said, see that paper's just a slip
that tells you, you can try.

A Harley's what she'd like to ride,
but there's no way that I would let her.
See, every Harley's got its pride,
a Honda would be better.

So, I bought her a Honda bike,
'Cause I figured she'd just smash it.
A Harley just would not be right
if she was gonna trash it.

Now you Honda riders out there,
please don't take offense.
It's your choice, I shouldn't care,
to you it must make sense.

See, I think those bikes made by Japan
might have a lot to give.
But, son, you gotta understand,
Japan ain't where I live.

'Cause when a Harley talks to me,
I understand with ease.
Ain't sure what language that might be,
but it ain't Japanese.

Well, anyhow the time arrived,
I gave her my best instructions.
Prayed to heaven she'd survive,
prepared to witness the destruction.

CARL STONE

She'd already tipped it over once,
when she'd just laid her hands upon it.
She said that didn't count because
she wasn't even on it.

And the engine wasn't goin'
and she wasn't in the road
and nobody would be knowin'
if the story wasn't told.

I nodded that I understood,
didn't let my feelin's show.
But this really can't be all that good
as far as omens go.

Her whole life passed through my mind,
at least the part of it I knew.
I recalled some of the good times,
and there'd been quite a few.

It would be a shame to lose her now,
after all that we'd been through.
But she was gonna do it anyhow,
wasn't much that I could do.

So, I put the dog and cat inside
and stepped back behind the truck.
Told her, "Go ahead and ride."
Then I wished her best of luck.

Her first take-off was fairly smooth.
She dragged her feet along.

But she was up and on the move,
Nothin' terrible was wrong.

Then she had some trouble steering,
she seemed to be too tense.
'Cause right then she started veering
right towards that barbed wire fence.

Now that fence, it is electrified.
And those barbs on it are sharp.
And if she crashed through on this ride,
Well it was gonna leave a mark.

I stepped out from behind the truck
to give a warning cry.
But the words, in my throat just stuck.
My mouth was parched and dry.

She was weaving way far to the right
and I knew gravity would win
when she brought that thing back upright
and swerved off down the road again!

I just stood there with my mouth agape.
Could not believe what I just saw.
Somehow that fence, she had escaped.
I'm still not sure just how.

I watched her wobble outta sight.
Didn't even bother now to chase her.
'Cause if she'd survived that first fright,
wasn't nothin' gonna phase her.

CARL STONE

When she reappeared there's somethin' strange.
What it was I couldn't tell.
'til she got closer within range.
Why, she's goin slow as hell!

Now that's something that I've never seen
in all my years with her.
Her ridin' along on a machine
when she wasn't just a blur.

I could see the fear deep in her eyes
but she'd made it back without a ding.
And that's when I first realized
she's gonna ride that thing!

Well, she told me she was scared to death.
She clutched the grips with knuckles white.
I just let out a long deep breath
and told her, "That's alright,"

'Cause now she knew what it was like,
and she'd learn to respect it.
'Cause things can happen on a bike
just when you least expect it.

So over country roads she follows me,
getting better every ride.
It won't be long, just wait and see
and we'll be ridin' side by side.

Oh, sometimes she'll hit a flowerpot
when she pulls on to the lawn.
She gets off, returns it to its spot

as if there's nothin' wrong.

But there's a nightmare that I sometimes see,
makes me wonder how I'll feel
when someday she snaps and screams by me
right up on her hind wheel.

Cause she's not a Harley Mama
but she's my Biker Babe.
If I can just get her off that Honda,
I think we'll have it made.

CARL STONE

> YA KNOW THE OLE SAYIN', THERE'S ONLY TWO THINGS IN LIFE THAT ARE CERTAIN, DEATH AND TAXES. I DON'T LIKE TO DWELL ALL TOO LONG ON EITHER ONE, BUT ON OCCASION I RUN ACROSS SOMEONE WHO DOES. THIS OLE FELLA WAS SURE HE WAS ABOUT TO DRAW HIS LAST BREATH.

GREEN BANANAS

March 16, 2002

I thought I should get off the farm,
one fine day in early spring.
So, I went to the local auction barn,
just to see what cows would bring.

Ole Joe leaned up against the door
soakin' up the sun's warm ray.
I'd seen him many times before,
thought I'd see what he had to say.

I told him that he looked real good,
he must have wintered very well.
When he straightened up right where he stood
said, "Nope, I've gone all to hell!"

He looked me straight into my eye,
spoke a line I'd never heard before.
"Ya see boy, I won't even buy
green bananas anymore."

"Yup, I'd say my end was near,

least I'm sure that's what I think.
Why, I don't even buy more beer
than I can sit and drink."

"Do ya' see this here ceegar, son?
Well, I'm gonna smoke it all.
I won't save half fer later on,
like I woulda done last fall."

"And I won't cut next year's wood supply,
like I've always done before.
'Cause, hell, I won't even buy
green bananas anymore."

"I won't fill my gas tank anymore,
get one gallon at a time.
Won't buy from that big discount store,
where I might hafta stand in line."

"Well, this year's garden, I won't try,
 of that I'm pretty sure.
'Cause, son, I won't even buy
green bananas anymore."

"Buy cheap batteries fer my light,
don't need no eveready bunny.
'Cause if they last beyond tonight,
'twould be just a waste of money."

"Yup my toes will soon point towards the sky,
I'll keep goin', ain't sure what for,
Did I tell ya', I don't even buy
green bananas anymore?"

CARL STONE

"You stand there with that silly grin,
as if you was immune!
Well, someday you'll be where I've been,
it'll happen all too soon!

I just slapped him on the shoulder
and headed on into the barn.
Somehow I felt a whole lot older
than when I'd just left the farm.

I didn't buy a thing that day,
Mostly visited with old friends.
Told them I would be on my way
as the sale came to an end.

And I heard Joe say to some poor guy
as I reached for my truck door,
"I tell ya' boy, I don't even buy,
green bananas anymore."

RURAL RAMBLINGS

HUNTING

December 1999

I knew that this would happen
each time I shot the gun.
I knew that all those misses
would give y'all some fun.

But that's the kinda guy I am.
I guess it's just my way.
I like to think of others
in all I do and say.

So I just shouldered up the gun
Kept jerkin on that trigger.
It'd be more than you could stand.
At least that's what I figured.

I coulda blamed the sunshine,
I coulda blamed the rain,
I coulda blamed it on the trees
that dotted the terrain.

I coulda blamed it on the fact
my shots were all downhill.
I coulda blamed in on the fact
that I was feeling ill.

I coulda blamed it on the shells,
or even on the gun.
But then I think that I'd spoiled

all of your guys fun.

I figured I'd just take the heat
for you who just can't shoot.
And everybody along the way
would have a laugh to boot.

Now some call me old nine shot,
Some snicker, ole dead eye.
Some just sit and laugh away
until I swear you'll cry.

But let a big ole buck come through,
you'll see a different man.
'Cause I'll drop him in his tracks
like you all know I can.

LUCKY LARRY

April 2013

Lucky Larry had a plan,
he always had some scheme.
But Larry was no normal man,
he reached out to grasp his dreams.

See, the price of eggs had raised a dime,
down at the local store,
and Larry had to draw the line,
wouldn't take it anymore.

His government had ripped him off,
his mechanic and his plumber.
He couldn't take it, that's enough,
least not from some chicken farmer.

He would buy twelve chickens of his own,
he was lucky as could be.
'Cause after he had got them home,
his eggs would all be free.

Now he'd have to build himself a shed,
so he ordered up the wood.
They brought it on a big flatbed,
his luck was holdin' good.

He marked those boards all true and straight,
this would take no time at all.
Everything was goin' great,

he reached for his new saw.

His hand somehow just seemed to slip
when he started up his saw.
Took off his fingertips,
didn't bother him at all.

"That was lucky" Larry said,
"My luck it never fails.
It could have been my thumb instead
then I couldn't hold the nails!"

After that the project went quite well,
his life was truly charmed,
'til off the roof poor Larry fell
and shattered his right arm.

"Well, that was lucky" Larry said
as he lay face down in the mud.
"Imagine if I'd hit my head,
could'a lost all my good luck."

Well Larry fin'ly got it built.
It cost more than he had planned.
Including all the doctor bills,
it totaled near four grand.

That was lucky, Larry thought,
as he tallied up the score.
There was a sale on stuff he'd bought,
it could have been much more.

Larry went to pick up his new hens

from a local chicken man,
and since he had no chicken pens,
took his wife's new minivan.

T'was not to long 'fore Larry found
things can sure get outta hand
with twelve grown chickens flyin' round
inside a minivan.

Hen feathers soon had filled the air,
'til Larry thought he'd choke.
He soon discovered then and there,
that chickens ain't housebroke.

There were chickens on the rearview mirror,
chickens on the dash,
chickens clear from front to rear.
Larry struggled not to crash.

He made it, home it wasn't far,
that chicken storm he'd weathered,
but when he rolled out of the car,
looked like he'd been tarred and feathered.

"That sure was lucky!" Larry cried.
"I could've had a wreck!
One of my chickens could've died,
she might have broke her neck!"

He finally got them in the barn
and locked them all inside.
It looked like none of them were harmed
from Larry's chicken ride.

CARL STONE

It was a week, or maybe more
when the first egg hit the pan.
You should have heard ole Larry roar,
"Take that you chicken man!"

"From now on my eggs are free!
How do you like me now?!
This all has worked so good for me
I'm thinking 'bout a cow!"

RURAL RAMBLINGS

RIDING MOWER

Fall 2001

It was just another dawn,
almost like any other.
But it was the day she'd mow the lawn,
and we'd all run for cover.

Now she had mowed the lawn before,
please don't get me wrong.
But this was different, that's for sure,
this time she'd ride along.

See, we'd always had a walk behind,
it didn't work too bad.
Besides the wife had lots of time,
and it was all she had.

Then she came home one sunny day,
from a sale just down the road.
Said she'd heard the neighbors say
their old rider they'd unload.

Fifty bucks was all, she said,
And it could be all mine.
And she could sit and ride instead
of walkin' all the time.

I couldn't see how this helped me.
Don't know why I got the urge.
Guess I love a deal, ya' see,

and figured I would splurge.

It was only twelve years old,
that's what the neighbor said.
The seat on it was black as coal,
the paint was shiny red.

Now every now and then in life,
you get more than just a deal.
Give the credit to the wife,
this mower was a steal.

I parked her right out in the grass,
for all the world to see.
I'd fin'ly got my own at last,
I was proud as I could be.

I even thought that from now on
I could give her a break.
Maybe now I'd mow the lawn.
She'd have more time to bake.

Guess she saw right through my plan,
said she was nobody's fool.
She could do the job at hand,
'sides I had chores to do.

So, I helped her get it goin',
then headed for the barn.
Guess she could do the mowin',
guess it couldn't do much harm.

From the barn I heard the hummin'.

RURAL RAMBLINGS

Couldn't stand it anymore,
thought I'd see how she was comin',
so I peeked out of the door.

What I witnessed next my friend,
wasn't for the faint of heart.
The picnic table stood on end.
The lawn chairs thrown apart.

The dog had dove beneath the truck.
The cat was up a tree.
Don't ya, know it, damn the luck,
she's headed straight for me!

She gripped the wheel, her knuckles white,
her hair was blown straight back.
I stood right there, froze with fright,
thought she was on attack.

The stones and dirt and grass just flew
as she whipped around a tree.
Guess right then was when I knew,
she wasn't really after me.

I guess common sense had all took wing,
hadn't thought of it so far.
Why, she was gonna drive that thing
same way she drives the car!

I just couldn't stand and stay,
couldn't bear to watch the crash.
I could only hope and pray
she'd soon run out of gas.

Then suddenly there was no sound.
The air was soft and still.
The cat crept back down to the ground.
I heard a robin's trill.

I slowly turned, surveyed the scene,
my throat sucked in a gasp.
She laid there by that red machine,
right face down in the grass.

Could it be she'd met her match?
Had this thing done her in?
Then she jumped up without a scratch
and hollered with a grin.

"This mower deck is plowin' sod,
I must've clipped that tree.
You'll prob'ly have to weld this rod.
Why don't you come and see?"

"Perhaps you drove a bit too fast.
You should be careful how you use it.
I'm afraid it just won't last
if you continue to abuse it."

"Why does this thing have a sixth gear?",
she all too quickly asked.
"Why would they even put it here,
if they thought it was too fast?"

I just turned and walked away.
I could not even talk.

RURAL RAMBLINGS

My thoughts drifted to a simpler day.
One where she was forced to walk.

STOLEN PIE

They say that on the other side
the grass is always greener,
They tell me that a stolen kiss
is one that's always sweeter.

But I am here to tell you
And I'm not sure just why,
That nothing tastes as good, I swear,
as a piece of stolen pie.

I didn't eat it right away,
I knew it wasn't right,
But I guess I always knew,
That I would lose the fight.

Now some men, they have honor,
Some men have standards high,
but I dare say, they've never faced,
some other person's pie.

Let's just say I faltered,
My morals all took wing.
Aw hell, I guess I'll tell ya',
I ate the whole damn thing!

Now I have lost my honor,
But it could get much worse,
I could end up the victim of
some ancient Polish curse.

RURAL RAMBLINGS

STORE BOUGHT BACON

You should be careful what you say,
to your girlfriend or your wife.
'Cause there could be a price to pay
that could change your way of life.

It happened on a sandy beach,
I can still recall it well.
And there's a lesson I will teach
in the story that I'll tell.

We spread a blanket on the sand,
we both had been in swimmin'.
My wife settled with a book in hand
and I lay back to watch the women.

Now, I didn't have a thing in mind,
it was just part of the view.
And she was havin' her good time,
I had nothin' else to do.

The bright sun was softened by a breeze,
'gainst the shore, the waves were lappin'.
My mind and body were at ease,
and then was when it happened!

Like a goddess, she rose from the waves,
a vision of delight.
And, I guess, boys, all's I can say,
she was put together right.

CARL STONE

She had, on her, an angel's face
with flowing, long blonde hair.
Everything was in its proper place,
all the way from there to there.

Her whole body bore the perfect tan,
her two piece suit just set it off.
And if you were a normal man,
to look away would sure be tough.

Her shapely legs were smooth and long.
She moved with style and grace.
She was kinda like an ole love song
from a different time and place.

See, guys, if there is a "10" out there,
then I'd say that she'd be it.
And if the men just stopped and stared,
well, she didn't mind a bit.

Now, I don't get off the farm too much,
So, this ain't a sight I'm used to seein'.
Oh, maybe on TV and such,
but not livin', movin', breathin'

Then, my wife looked up from her book
and I guess she caught me gawkin',
'cause she gave me an awful look
before she started talking.

"She won't clean and feed your hogs, no chance,
the way I do for you,"

RURAL RAMBLINGS

I answered, still deep in my trance,
"Don't believe I'd ask her to."

Heh... We don't raise pigs anymore.
See, I ain't got time to clean the pen.
We buy our pork chops at the store,
that's how it's been since then.

So, be cautious with your words, ya' see,
sure of the statements you are makin'
'Cause you could wind up just like me,
eatin' store bought bacon.

CARL STONE

WATER SLIDE

I know it was quite some time back,
the kids were pretty small,
but I will tell this close to fact,
the best I can recall.

The family had all done their part,
puttin' up next winter's hay,
so before the mutiny could start
I thought we should get away.

I tried to grab a day or two,
sometimes maybe three,
and give them somethin' fun to do
and somethin' new to see.

We all would pile into the car
and head for the open road.
We never traveled all that far,
but the times we had were good.

There was this park, it was brand new,
with a long twisting water slide.
It seemed like just the thing to do,
thought we'd all enjoy the ride.

So, soon we gathered at the base
of this monstrous water slide.
Ready now for our first taste
of that grand and glorious ride.

RURAL RAMBLINGS

It depended on your expertise
on which slide that you should go.
One for kids and retirees,
the big one for the pro.

Now, my prowess as an athlete
was rather legendary.
This couldn't be that great a feat,
it couldn't be that scary.

So I headed straight up to the top
as if I was a pro.
Made sure the wife and children stopped
at the kiddie slide below.

This here slide is pretty fast
the man behind me said.
And "What would be your name?", I asked.
He replied that it was Ted.

Now Ted, he was a giant man,
both tall and big around,
and if I guess as best I can
he weighed at least three hundred pounds.

"Is there a special trick to it?",
I politely asked of him.
"Just grab that pad and stick to it",
he answered with a grin.

I sat down on this plastic pad
and started on my run.

CARL STONE

This wasn't gonna be that bad,
I was really havin' fun!

I was whizzin' halfway down
when I think I caught my toe,
'cause suddenly I spun around,
and I began to roll!

These slides aren't made for that at all,
I found that out pretty quick,
'cause the thuds when I bounced off the wall
would make a grown man sick.

I fin'lly came to rest at last
when I crashed around a bend.
I thought the worst had surely passed,
my bouncing reached its end.

I lay there, clutching to the sides
when I heard this rumbling sound.
That was when I realized,
BIG TED WAS COMING DOWN!

Yup, Big Ted was right behind me
and if he hit me with full force,
they'd be lucky just to find me,
never recognize the corpse.

I scrambled for my little pad,
pushed off with all my might.
Well folks, I gave it all I had,
wouldn't die without a fight.

RURAL RAMBLINGS

The bottom pool, I hit it runnin',
skimmed across it like a jet,
'cause I knew Big Ted was comin'
and he hadn't caught me yet!

I sat there, gasping, on the bank,
still in a fair amount of pain,
and the Good Lord I was about to thank,
when I heard the wife complain.

"You know, you're having all the fun,
I think we should switch off.
I wanna ride the big one,
I'm sure it ain't that tough."

Now, there are decisions you must make
when you become a man.
And there are paths that you must take
to lend a helping hand.

"There ain't no real trick to it,"
I tried to force a grin.
"Just grab that pad and stick to it,
right to the very end."

You know, it's gotta be that blonde thing,
that's all I've got to say.
'Cause she slid down that thing
three more times that day.

CARL STONE

> I'VE BEEN A DEER HUNTER ALL MY LIFE. A LARGE PART OF THE FUN IS THE CAMARADERIE AND JOKING THAT GOES ON WITH MY FELLOW HUNTERS. THIS IS THE STORY OF ONE SUCH HUNT.

OLE ONE SHOT

December 2002

I'll tell you people right up front,
When I go huntin' deer,
It ain't always just about the hunt,
it's the stories that you hear.

Now, some say that I exaggerate,
make a log out of a twig.
That statement ain't quite fair to make,
I just remember big!

Two young men said, "There's a small buck,
He lays up there on that hill,
And maybe with a lot of luck,
we could make a kill."

"It will be hard to sneak on him,
what with all that thick brush,
maybe we should get more men,
with radios and such."

"I s'pect it's just a one man chore,"
the young fellas heard me say.
"I suppose you could round up some more,

RURAL RAMBLINGS

if they don't get in my way."

"See, if you promise not to spook him,
I'll just take this here gun,
and walk up there and shoot him,
if it won't spoil your fun."

"But you don't have no camo
you're just wearin' old barn clothes,
and you don't have no radio,
you won't know where he goes."

"I think you've missed the point, son,
'cause when I get up there,
if it's just me and this ole gun,
he won't **go** nowhere!"

So they each went and picked a spot,
case I should fail in my attack.
They thought that I might miss the shot.
What would be the odds of that?

And, I circled up, way around,
'til the wind was in my face,
and quietly I started down,
to find his hidin' place.

Now, when I say that I move quiet,
I fear that you won't understand.
So, I'll try now to describe it,
the very best I can.

Like the morning dew that crashes

CARL STONE

into the meadow grass,
or the ray of sun that smashes
off a shining piece of glass.

Or the deaf'ning thundrous quake
of a leaf floating to the road.
These are like the sounds I make
when I'm in my stalking mode.

I crept up over this small hump,
Where a doe had chose to lay.
I gently slapped her on the rump
to send her on her way.

For she was not my quarry,
no, she was not my prey.
She didn't have to worry,
she would live another day.

Cause that young buck lay up ahead,
right in the thickest part
and soon a piece of red-hot lead
Would pierce his brave young heart.

To aim this gun, it would be tough,
down where the brush was thicker.
'Cause he'd be movin' fast enough,
I just knew I must be quicker.

See, I'm as quick as I am quiet,
Believe it or not,
And soon he'd have to try it.
That's when I'd get my shot.

RURAL RAMBLINGS

It all ended in a blinding flash,
I had time for once quick shot.
The deer took off in a dash,
but I was sure he'd drop.

He scrambled, then took one last leap.
I'm sure he did the best he could.
Then fell dead into a heap,
just like I knew he would,

This was done by one lone guy,
'gainst one wily whitetail buck.
One gun, one shot, one steady eye,
and this deer ran out of luck.

It all had happened like I said
Back when we'd all begun,
If you gotta deer that you want dead,
send just me and this ole gun.

Now, this story, it may differ some,
if it's told by a beginner.
But I guess that it don't matter none,
I'm eatin' venison for dinner.

CARL STONE

CHARLIE

I won't give his real name,
I'll just call him Charlie.
But the bike on which the fella came,
Well, it was not a Harley.

He slipped quietly into the drive
on his slick two-wheeled machine.
About the luckiest man alive,
or at least that's how it seemed.

'Cause that lady up behind him
was as fine as she could be.
Whatever she could find in him
sure got the best of me.

It could've been the bike, I s'pose
that attracted her to Charlie.
I s'pect the Good Lord only knows
'cause the bike was not a Harley.

Anyway, I was glad they came .
It was good to see them there
'cause good friends, by any name,
sometimes it seems are rare.

We sat and chatted for awhile
and had a laugh or two.
When he said he had to make a mile
'cause they had things to do.

RURAL RAMBLINGS

So they got up and went outside
and mounted on their steed.
Ready now to take a ride,
they both looked fine indeed!

"Sure runs quiet," I would say,
"It ain't runnin'"", he replied.
And that was when I feared that day
the poor ole bike had died.

This was no time to think up jokes,
to throw at sad ole Charlie,
but did I mention to you folks,
his bike was not a Harley?

Well, we started peelin' fiberglass
so we could get a look,
and finally we even asked
the girls to read the book.

But alas, all hope had passed us by,
that engine would not roll
no matter what we seemed to try
the darn thing wouldn't go.

There was talk that they could leave it here,
that idea, well, I fought it.
Someone might drive by I feared,
and think that I bought it.

I said, "Let's push it toward the hill
then you just pop the clutch.

CARL STONE

It'll run; I know it will –
you got that special touch."

So we pushed it just a few short feet
when that engine came alive.
It purred so smooth it sounded sweet.
She climbed on the back to ride.

As I watched 'em ride on outta sight
I just stood there and smiled.
Thinkin' then 'bout what I'd write
when I got a little while.

I hope my Harley never breaks,
but I fear someday it will.
I sure hope that all it takes
is a shove down off this hill.

THIS NEXT PIECE TAKES US DOWN A LITTLE DIFFERENT PATH. I WAS INVITED TO A MURDER MYSTERY PARTY IN WHICH WE ALL WERE TO ASSUME PRE-ASSIGNED ROLES. MINE WAS THAT OF A RATHER UNSCRUPULOUS, FREE-THINKING POET. I WROTE THIS FOR THAT PARTY. READ CAREFULLY, AS EACH READERS INTERPRETATION TELLS A GOOD DEAL ABOUT ONE'S INNERMOST THOUGHTS.

SAILING

Margarita was the name
that she so proudly wore
and I was staggered by her beauty
as I strolled along the shore.

I could see her tugging gently
on her lines tied to the dock,
begging for her freedom
with every subtle rock.

Her silky sails fluttered
in the everchanging wind,
and she beckoned me to free her
and her passions deep within.

I reached down and untied her,
though I was not her owner.
I felt we could go places
no one else had ever shown her.

CARL STONE

The voyage at first was gentle
as we headed out to sea.
She seemed to be enjoying
the fact that she was free.

The ride soon became violent.
She began to lunge and buck.
I knew for me to stay with her
would take a bit of luck.

Wave after wave crashed o'er us.
I could feel the surging foam.
It ended in a shudder and a
long and joyous moan.

I lay there clutching to her,
both of us completely spent.
The storm that rose so slowly,
all too swiftly it had went.

I steered her back into the bay.
No one else had ever seen us.
What happened out there on that sea
would always be between us.

Margarita was the name
that she so proudly wore
and I was staggered by her beauty
as I strolled along the shore.

Shame on you.
It was a boat ride, just a damn boat ride!

MUSINGS

CARL STONE

TURNING FIFTY

March 2000

I turned fifty just the other day,
and I took my share of kiddin'.
It seems the real facts of life,
from some are sadly hidden.

Nature has its own cruel way
of sheltering the truth.
She rarely lets it show itself
to those that have their youth.

Now, if I am over the hill,
at least I've made the climb.
It's gotta mean I was on top,
somewhere back in time.

And I'd rather be a "has been"
than be a "never was",
but back there when I was on top,
shouldn't there have been applause?

If there was, I failed to hear it,
failed to see the banners fly.
The day that I was at my peak,
just somehow passed me by.

Was it back there twenty years
or thirty years ago?
Somewhere in between, I'd guess,

RURAL RAMBLINGS

I'll prob'ly never know.

So those of you that think that you
are nowhere near your prime,
you could be absolutely right,
you may have passed your time.

CARL STONE

> **CHANGE—A CHANGE RECENTLY ENTERED MY LIFE, ONE THAT WAS STRONGLY ENCOURAGED BY BOTH MY WIFE AND KIDS. SOME HAVE CALLED IT MY SECOND CHILDHOOD, OTHERS A MIDLIFE CRISIS. I MOST OFTEN REFER TO IT AS EARLY STAGES OF SENILITY. SEE, IN MY YOUTH I DROVE A HARLEY-DAVIDSON MOTORCYCLE. AFTER OVER THIRTY YEARS, THE OLE URGE WAS COMIN' BACK. THIS IS THAT STORY.**

THE HARLEY

July 2003

I stood there in the Harley shop
at the age of fifty-three.
I s'pose it was too late to stop,
don't know what come over me.

I told myself to get out now,
Just walk out and go on home.
But I'd been mesmerized somehow
by all that gleaming chrome.

It'd been thirty years since I had rode,
But that ole feelin' never leaves ya'.
If you told me I had lost control,
well, I guess I would believe ya'.

'Cause I told the man "I'll take her."
And put down a hundred bucks.
"You guys make out the papers,
I'll be back to pick her up."

RURAL RAMBLINGS

I walked out the door, almost in tears
with about a mile wide grin.
Finally, after all those years,
I was a Harley man again.

Somewhere between the shop and car,
reality sunk in.
I could not believe I'd come this far
or the mess I now was in.

'Cause there was one thing to say the least,
one fact, I couldn't hide it.
Now that I'd bought this shiny beast,
I was sure I couldn't ride it.

It was way too much machine
and it had been so long.
Everything about it seemed
so crazy and so wrong.

I didn't sleep too well that night.
My rest was filled with dreams
of broken bones and twisted bikes
and other awful scenes.

But fear is really not a choice
when you're a Harley man.
You must ignore that inner voice
and just ride it, best you can.

My wife told me that I'd be fine,
offered up her reassurance.

CARL STONE

Why was she spending all that time
thumbin' through my life insurance?

Well, when I went down to pick it up
Harley had their road show there.
The parkin lot, just my luck,
looked like the county fair

There was trucks and cars and bikes and vans,
They even had a hot dog wagon.
Men and women holdin' hands
Of the kids that they were draggin'.

All thoughts of me just sneakin' out
right then seemed pretty wild.
I'd be doing good to leave without
maiming some poor child.

I know why Knievel jumped those cars,
we all have seen him do it.
It would be easier by far
than tryin' to ride on through it.

But fear is really not a choice
when you're a Harley man.
You must ignore that inner voice
and just RIDE IT, best you can.

So, I told 'em "Point it toward the street,
way across that parkin' lot."
And I settled down into the seat
and I fired that monster up.

RURAL RAMBLINGS

That ole rumble down between my knees,
Well, it took me back in time.
I slipped it into gear with ease,
felt a chill run up my spine.

I let the clutch out real smooth,
'til I felt it take ahold.
GOOD LORD, the thing began to move!
I was up and on the go.

I'd stared out upon my fight
like a sailor out on leave,
struggling to stay upright
as I wobbled and I weaved.

OH LORD, don't let me hit her,
that child so young and sweet!
I'll no longer be a sinner,
If you'll just get me to the street.

The rest went by in just a whirl
as I look back upon it now.
I guess I must have missed the girl
and got to the street somehow.

I worked my way on out of town
without a single hitch.
A quiet county road I found,
where wild daisies lined the ditch.

A place where dark green corn was growin'
and the air was brisk and pure,
with some ole farmer out there mowin'

CARL STONE

like his daddy did before.

A place where all you feel is breeze.
And I'd forgotten how that feels.
With the Harley rumble 'tween your knees
and the road beneath your wheels.

I'd say I felt I was back home,
long before I reached the house,
'cause rollin' down that country road
can't compare to nothin' else.

My wife now thinks that she should have
a Harley of her own.
I swallow hard, I do not laugh,
don't even sit and groan.

See, fear is really not a choice
when you're a Harley man.
Just listen to your woman's voice
and cope the best you can.

RURAL RAMBLINGS

OLD MAN WINTER

The old man raised a gnarled knuckle,
as he rapped firmly on our door.
He let out a low and raspy chuckle
as we let him in once more.

His crippled body old and bent,
determined steps were short and slow.
It seemed where e'er the old man went
swirled an eerie rush of cold.

With snapping knees and cracking hips
the old man shuffled in.
Looking closely at his cold cracked lips
you could see a gleeful grin.

He scuffed his way cross the room
to a big stuffed easy chair.
He settled in and way too soon
seemed like he'd stay right there.

That was way back in November.
The date I don't recall.
The one thing I do remember,
it was the end of fall.

Right through the holidays he stayed
s'pose he gave a special touch.
Anyway, he was behaved,
nobody minded much.

CARL STONE

It was sometime back in February
we all started to believe,
that though the thought was scary,
he just might never leave!

Mid-March he struggled to his feet
as if he was to go.
Alas, he stumbled to his seat,
gazed out at falling snow.

Today in April he arose
and headed for the door.
In his heart he knew, I suppose,
that he could stay no more.

He may swing by again
some blustery spring day.,
but he won't knock to be let in.
He knows that he can't stay.

Old Man Winter is his name
in case you haven't guessed.
Next fall he'll be back just the same,
to live as our house guest.

The old man raised a gnarled knuckle,
as he rapped firmly on our door.
He let out a low and raspy chuckle
as we let him in once more.

RURAL RAMBLINGS

CHRISTMAS IN AMERICA

2007

Christmas day is drawing near,
it's hard to miss the signs.
Glasses full of Christmas cheer,
bright lights and party times.

Santa Claus is on the streets,
spreading Christmas joy.
His sleigh piled high with Christmas treats
for every girl and boy.

Shoppers now have swarmed the store,
pushing and shoving their way through.
With little thought of nothing more
than the buying they must do.

Fights erupt over special dolls
when the last ones leave the shelves.
Weary shoppers fill the malls,
thinking only of themselves.

Trees are strapped on top of cars,
angry drivers' horns are blarin'.
Party-goers pack the bars
to keep the good times goin'.

Lights! The lights are everywhere,
indeed, they are breath-takin',
but most people really do not care

'bout the message they are makin'.

Glitz and glitter everywhere,
grand huge mounds of food.
Bells and whistles fill the air
to get us in the mood.

Our schools will have a holiday,
whatever it is worth,
being careful not to say
it's about our Savior's birth.

My goodness, what did I just say?
Did I offend someone?
To mention that this holiday
is the birth of God's own Son.

It's alright to have a real good time,
we indeed should celebrate,
but this country needs to step in line,
before it is too late.

So, let's remember this my friend,
It's about our savior's birth!
Let's show our own good will toward men
and strive for peace on earth.

> NOW, I SHOULD STATE RIGHT UP FRONT, I HAVEN'T HELD A REAL JOB IN THIRTY YEARS, SO I AM COMPLETELY UNQUALIFIED TO SPEAK OR WRITE ON THIS NEXT SUBJECT. BUT THAT HAS NEVER STOPPED ME BEFORE, SO WHY WOULD IT NOW. A FRIEND WAS HAVING WHAT COULD BE TERMED AS A PERSONALITY CONFLICT WITH HIS BOSS AT WORK. IT WAS A DIFFERENT VERSION OF THE SAME OLE STORY I'VE HEARD FOR YEARS FROM A LOT OF YOU POOR WORKING PEOPLE. I WOULD NOT HOWEVER GIVE A COPY OF THIS TO YOUR OWN BOSS WITHOUT FIRST LINING UP OTHER EMPLOYMENT.

BIG DOG

Yup, you are the "Big Dog,"
on the porch up by the door,
the mangy curs beneath you
just sit and beg for more.

You've climbed the business ladder,
gettin' closer to the top.
How ya' got there doesn't matter,
you say jump, your people hop.

There is one thing to know for sure,
while you're countin' all your loot,
the dog that lies next to the door,
feels first the master's boot.

Them other dogs can just lie there,
do nought but scratch and lick.

CARL STONE

The big man he don't even care,
it's your butt that he'll kick.

The squirrel highest in the tree
 when the woodsman cuts it down,
will have the biggest fall, you see,
before he hits the ground.

I guess its sorta nature's way,
any other would be wrong.
He should have the most to pay
that hears the sweetest song.

The mouse he answers to the cat,
the cat unto the dog.
The dog unto his master,
that master unto God.

RURAL RAMBLINGS

> WHEN WE HAD THE BIG BLACKOUT SOME TIME BACK, IT GOT ME TO THINKING. THERE ARE A FEW CONSTANTS IN LIFE THAT WE TAKE FOR GRANTED. WHAT IF THAT CHANGED?

THE BLACKOUT

August 2003

A while back we had a blackout,
All across the great northeast
and lotsa people went without,
I s'pose to say the least.

But they all knew the sun would rise
and brighten their next day.
Now wouldn't they all be surprised
if it didn't happen quite that way.

What if the sun just burnt out?
I mean, just plumb run outta fuel?
It could happen with no doubt,
You think different, you're a fool!

'Cause all the sources that I've asked
tell me it's life is long,
not to worry, it will last,
but what if they're wrong?

See, that sun's about ninety-three
million miles away,
and how they know how long it'd be?

CARL STONE

Heh I'm afraid I just can't say.

So those of you that like to fret,
lay your old worries to one side.
I've got for you the best one yet,
should keep you occupied.

Cause it takes eight minutes for sunlight
to reach us, anyhow.
So you don't know, I might be right,
it could be out right now.

A while back we had a blackout
that put some people in a bind.
But I'll tell ya, when the sun goes out,
Heh, it's gonna blow their mind!

I AM STILL HERE ANYWAY

March 17, 2012

It started back 'fore I could walk,
I was just a little kid.
I cut my teeth, if I recall,
chewin' lead paint off my crib.

Pretty soon they put me on the floor,
I was big enough to crawl.
There were those days when I got bored,
I ate the plaster off the wall.

That plaster, it stuck in your throat,
but I'd wash it down somehow
with the bottle that I'd brought
of raw milk right from the cow.

Rode my bike when I got older,
back then the roads were dirt.
Sometimes I'd lose it on the shoulder –
Good Lord those crashes hurt.

I didn't wear protective gear,
weren't no helmets way back then.
I just pedaled hard, with no fear,
right to the very end.

Pretty soon I went to climbin' trees,
s'pose you know how that turned out.
As I came crashin' through the leaves

CARL STONE

I learned what gravity's about.

I rode back in a pickup bed,
there weren't no seatbelt there.
Sat on a sack of feed instead
with wind blowin' through my hair.

I played cowboy in my childhood dreams
as I crouched behind a log
and I've kneeled and drank right from streams
where I'd just caught a frog.

I'd play shirtless in the sun
to try and get a tan.
Sometimes I'd just break free and run
with scissors in my hand.

All these things might help explain
'bout the way I am today.
Don't s'pose I will complain,
'cause I'm still here anyway.

> SOMETIMES IN MY ZEAL TO EXPAND MY IMAGINATIVE POWERS I MAY STEP PRECARIOUSLY CLOSE TO THE EDGE OF SCIENTIFIC REALITY. HOWEVER, AFTER DISCUSSING THIS NEXT CONCEPT WITH ONE OF THE MORE RECOGNIZED AND RESPECTED SCIENTIFIC MINDS OF OUR TIME, WE AGREED. THERE IS A DISTINCT POSSIBILITY THAT SOME OF THE MOLECULES THAT COMPRISE OUR AIR SUPPLY TODAY COULD HAVE INDEED BEEN AROUND FOR AND INDEFINITELY LONG PERIOD OF TIME. WITH THAT ASSURANCE IN MIND, I PROCEEDED TO WRITE THIS.

NOTHING MORE THAN AIR

January 6, 2002

A gentle breeze brushes your face,
runs its finger through your hair.
Overcoming time and space,
it's nothing more than air.

It's not yours to ponder where
this puff of wind has been.
For it is nothing more than air
just coming 'round again.

How many ages has it traveled,
encircling this sphere?
How many lives has it unraveled
before it passed through here?

Perhaps it cooled the Savior's brow

by the Sea of Galilee.
And does the same thing even now
as it caresses thee.

Did it pump water from the Nile
to quench a Pharaoh's thirst?
Or carry bubbles from a child
skyward till they burst?

Did it sculpt the dunes of sand
on some desert long ago?
And does it now, with the same hand,
carve out a drift of snow?

Once did it carry in the rain
to an arid, sunbaked land?
And then proceed to grind the grain
to stave off starvation's hand?

Did its gusts propel a craft
across a sea unknown,
and safely bring its huddled mass
to a new and glorious home?

Was it not once a portion
of some ancient vicious gale,
leaving corpses in the ocean,
tearing at a vessel's sails?

Or did it clear the smoke away
from a field in Gettysburg
as people wept in sad dismay
at what they saw and heard?

Did it hold aloft the bird of war
O'er a distant far east land
that shook the earth like n'ere before
and changed the course of man?

It might have ravaged some poor soul
as it stripped him of his home
and when the twister ceased to blow
left him weeping and alone.

And did it fan the forest flame
that ran its course at last
and left a body with no name,
reducing it to ash?

So is it that of angel's breath
still sweet from heaven's shore?
Or does it bring the stench of death
from Satan's evil roar?

A gentle breeze brushes your face,
runs its finger through your hair.
Overcoming time and space,
it's nothing more than air.

CARL STONE

> **FOR YOU LADIES OUT THERE THAT FEEL YOU HAVE THE ONLY HUSBAND IN THE WORLD THAT'S REAL SLACKER... WELL, THIS IS FOR YOU.**

THE WOODPILE'S GETTING SMALLER

March 2002

Well, the woodpile's getting smaller,
the darkness is losin' length.
The ole sun is getting taller,
the cold has lost its strength.

The coolness of the morning wind
reminds us of where we've been,
but the ice it forms is pretty thin,
spring is on its way again.

The cold-weather projects on my list,
that I drew up last fall,
well, most of them I guess I missed,
what with holidays and all.

To start them now would be too late,
at least that's what I fear.
Suppose that list will have to wait,
'til cold comes 'round next year.

Yup, the woodpile's getting smaller,
snow of white is turning brown.
Soon the lawn will green with color,
still those projects won't be done.

RURAL RAMBLINGS

I can feel myself begin to tire,
just thinking 'bout such things.
I guess I'll sit here by the fire
and start my list for spring.

CARL STONE

WATER

I don't get off the farm too much,
most all I need's right here.
Some folks would say I'm outta touch,
they could be right, I fear.

'Cause there's somethin' goin' on out there,
that I don't understand.
There's people goin' mad, I swear,
and it's getting outta hand.

Why, there's people payin' money,
for water in a bottle.
And to me that sure seems funny,
but they charge the stores full throttle.

See, they began to advertise it
and have sales on the stuff.
And, before they realized it,
they just couldn't get enough!

It was like they'd found a whole new drink,
and folks couldn't wait to try it.
They never took the time to think,
they just rushed out to buy it.

Now, I'll pay for soda and for beer,
See, somebody had to make it.
But when I want water around here,
I walk to the sink and take it!

RURAL RAMBLINGS

Downtown I heard some folks say
which BRAND it was they preferred.
I quickly turned and walked away
so my laughter wasn't heard.

In big cities there are bars they say,
and I s'pose its prob'ly true,
where if you're dumb enough to pay,
they'll sell oxygen to you.

Still, I'll tip my hat to the guy,
that's smart enough to see,
that some people will rush out to buy
what they can get for free.

I'll stay here on the farm, I guess,
right here's where you'll find me.
Where I'll never know which water's best
and my oxygen is free!

CARL STONE

PHONES

I remember when the telephone
hung right there on the wall,
and you had to be right there at home
to take or make a call.

See when that phone began to ring,
there's no panic, none at all,
didn't have to try and find the thing,
it just hung there, on the wall.

It wouldn't take a single photograph,
couldn't text or browse at all.
There was just one use that it could have,
to take or make a call.

And if it rang and we weren't home,
 no machine was there to take it.
Good Lord, without the modern phone,
how did we ever make it?

RURAL RAMBLINGS

THE FOOTBALL GAME

January 26, 1998

The game was all decided,
by experts near and far,
there was no way John Elway
could ever beat Brett Favre.

But could the faith of one lone fan
provide the inspiration,
for Elway and the Broncos
to shock the entire nation?

At halftime, Dick, I clutched my chest,
was truly frightened,
could it be you really knew?
You truly were enlightened?

Then came the second half,
my pulse began to slow,
Green Bay quickly tied it up,
they'd win this Super Bowl.

But on came big John Elway,
he would not be denied.
He ran, he passed and when he's
done the score's no longer tied.

Again my heart began to race,
I thought about my dollar,
I leapt up from my easy chair
and I began to holler!

CARL STONE

Somehow Green Bay felt my pain,
They knew about my grief,
out they came, charged down and tied,
much to my relief.

Relief soon turned to anguish
Joy soon turned to pain
Elway wasn't gonna quit,
he went out and scored again.

Then suddenly Denver won it,
I can't believe such luck,
I can't believe that damn John
Elway just cost me a buck.

So let's all toast John Elway,
let's all shout his name!
Or let's not, just say we did,
after all it's just a game.

KIDS CLOTHES

Now what about the sneakers craze?
Just when did that begin?
Way back in my good ole days
you just wore 'em in the gym.

You didn't wear 'em in the street,
that's not what they were for.
You only put 'em on your feet
to grip the ole gym floor.

And out there all those baseball caps,
wouldn't kids now be surprised?
To find they put visors on those hats
to keep sun out of their eyes.

With visors worn to side or back,
well, it just ain't gonna work.
Now add to that the simple fact,
you might look like a jerk.

I won't buy a car that's full of rust
or new tires bald and worn,
but there are those that feel they must
buy their jeans pre-ripped and torn.

But those baggy pants are still the worst –
look just like a bunch of clowns.
In my days that was just the curse
of wearing hand-me-downs.

CARL STONE

As I view the kids new styles and ways
I still ponder how they got 'em.
My mind drifts to those finer days
and a pair of striped bell-bottoms.

RURAL RAMBLINGS

INSIDE YOUR OWN FRONT DOOR

"If that business deal had just gone through,"
the man mattered to his wife.
"If I'd only not been such a fool,
we'd all be set for life."

He sat at his kitchen table,
his hands wrapped 'round his achin' head,
so distraught he's barely able
to hear what his woman said.

"S'pose it don't hurt to follow dreams
and always search for more,
but you look right past, sometimes, it seems
what's inside your own front door."

"We've never felt a hunger pain
when we climbed the stairs to bed.
We've never slept out in cold rain
with this roof over our head."

"We have always had clothes to wear
though sometimes a wee bit tattered,
and family gathered round who care.
Guess we've had all that really mattered."

"I think that in your search for more
you should remember those with less,
and one thing you should do for sure –
Thank God that we've been blessed."

IN THE NEWS

> **NOW, I HAVE BEEN A LITTLE RELUCTANT TO ADMIT IT IN THE PAST, BUT IN THE FIGHT OF RECENT EVENTS I'LL COME RIGHT OUT AND CONFESS. I DON'T HAVE A PORTFOLIO. ALMOST ALL MY INVESTMENTS, LIKE MANY OTHER FARMERS, I SUPPOSE, I CAN REACH OUT AND TOUCH. MY STOCK IS A DIFFERENT KIND—ITS GOT FOUR LEGS AND A TAIL.**

STOCKS

January 15, 2001

I heard that stocks are plungin',
it'll soon affect us all.
Well, it ain't got me lungin'
for the phone there on the wall.

See, I am just a common man,
I 'spose I'm outta touch.
If it don't deal with cows or land,
then it don't mean too much.

All my stock is cowhide bound,
slickest fit you've ever seen,
and they will raise themselves, I've found,
on pastures lush and green.

Sure, I've seen mine take a dip. . .
in the pond behind the barn,
and even if they slide or slip,
don't seem to do much harm.

CARL STONE

My cards are on the table
It's a pretty good strong hand.
So I'll farm while I'm still able.
Got the cows, I own the land.

Yup, all the stock that I call mine,
Gives me milk and meat.
Way I see it, down the line,
even brokers gotta eat.

THE OLYMPICS

February 1998

I've been watching the Olympics
being held at Nagano.
And to comment quite frankly,
it's really quite a show.

The men & women swishing
on all that snow & ice,
is really quite impressive,
they all do look so nice.

But I've gotta tell ya',
and this I must report,
there are a few of these events
that I just can't call sport.

To call them entertainment
would surely be alright,
to watch them spin & twirl on skates
and jump with all their might.

But every time I've watched them
I see no ref at all.
They are out there all alone
and where the hell's the ball?

Now I can find no goal line,
no basket or home plate.
"How do you get to score?", I ask,

"when all you do is skate?"

The judges, they assure me,
know the score for all these tricks,
are they the same one that came up
with a perfect score of six?

Now they must watch real close
to tell a triple from a double,
and if they blink at the wrong time
I'd say they were in trouble.

Now if I was a judge and knew
I'd missed it by a mile,
I'd look straight at the skater
and check out her cute smile.

And if she was smiling,
just like she did before,
I'd figure she just did it right,
give her a perfect score.

Double axles, triple lutz,
spins & jumps and such,
all these terms to me
just don't mean too much.

To me I just can't call this sport,
it's simply art, that's all.
'Cause after all how can you score
with no timeclock and no ball?

Now next time you're home late guys,

RURAL RAMBLINGS

and think you're in a fix,
just tell her, "In my eyes dear,
you'll always be a six."

And as you're flying backwards
out of your home sweet home,
maybe you can spin
a double axle of your own.

CARL STONE

LEGACY OF MCVEIGH

Tim, oh Tim, what have you done?
What brought you to this place?
You were but just one father's son
whose name you would disgrace.

The cause you sought to further,
You set back for countless years.
For somewhere in your fervor
you verified their fears.

Now, should I choose myself to arm
what would be the peoples thought?
They fear that I would do them harm
since the havoc that you've wrought.

People's lives went up in flame
outside a Texas town
You have used their name in vain,
stomped their souls into the ground.

From heavens they will curse your name
when they see what you have done.
You would have them share your shame,
but they were peaceful ones.

The only justice I see now
is not that of your death,
but that the truth you knew somehow
'ere you drew your final breath.

RURAL RAMBLINGS

Tim, oh Tim, what have you done?
What brought you to this place?
You were but just one father's son
whose name you would disgrace.

CARL STONE

> THE EVENTS OF SEPTEMBER 11, 2001, LEFT ME CONFUSED, STUNNED, ANGERED, AND SADDENED. I TRIED SEVERAL TIMES TO WRITE ABOUT IT, TO MAKE SENSE OF THE SENSELESS, TO FIND GOOD IN THE EVIL, TO BRING SOME SUNSHINE INTO THE GLOOM. I CAME UP EMPTY. IT WAS OVER A MONTH LATER THAT I WROTE THIS, STILL SHOWING A MEASURE OF DISBELIEF. I CANNOT UNDERSTAND THIS KIND OF HATRED, ESPECIALLY WHEN SHROUDED IN A PEOPLE'S RELIGIOUS BELIEFS. EVEN FANATICISM MOST GENERALLY HAS A HOLY IDEAL AT ITS CORE; I CAN FIND NONE IN THIS MOST UNHOLY ACT.

9-11-01

October 29, 2001

I've heard the speeches that were wrote.
The songs have all been sung.
I've listened to the prayers they spoke.
The bells have all been rung.

So do I stand here all alone
In dumbfounded disbelief,
that a people we have never known
could cause us all such grief?

Twas not knives that did the killing,
and it wasn't just airplanes.
The thought to me most chilling,
it was done by human brains.

RURAL RAMBLINGS

What on earth could spawn such hate?
From a distant far-off land?
Why did we recognize, too late,
the true evil of this man?

For years we've done our daily chores,
encased inside our bubbles.
Given little thought to wars
or other third world troubles.

What happened over there each day
didn't really matter much.
I guess it would be safe to say
that we were out of touch.

Yes, other people lived in fear -
ours was a different story.
That could never happen here -
not underneath Ole Glory.

Then one day our land of peace,
Shattered like a boom of thunder.
Our solace from earth's evil reach
was swiftly torn asunder.

The freedoms we felt were our right
made us an easy mark.
They hit us when the sun shone bright
didn't even wait till dark.

They caught us with our pants down
right around our knees,
then hit the softest spot they found,

and did it all with ease.

They gave us a sucker punch I
in no uncertain terms.
Security was out to lunch,
so they followed up with germs.

So now our bubble has been popped.
We've felt the devil's hand.
Those that did this must be stopped.
United we will stand.

To go to Alllah in the sky,
dreams one frightened evil man.
I s'pose it's up to us to try
to help him all we can!

> SINCE SEPTEMBER ELEVENTH, HOMELAND SECURITY HAS BECOME A TOP PRIORITY FOR OUR GOVERNMENT. SECURITY MEASURES AT OUR AIRPORTS HAVE BECOME BOTH EXPENSIVE AND TIME CONSUMING. NOW, I CAME UP WITH AN IDEA THAT I FIGURED WOULD DETER TERRORISTS AND SPEED UP THOSE LONG LINES IN THE TERMINALS. BEFORE I TOOK IT TO THE AUTHORITIES, HOWEVER, I RAN IT BY MY WIFE. IT WENT SOMETHIN' LIKE THIS.

FLIGHT SECURITY

April 2002

Now days we're spending funds,
and usin' lotsa time,
to keep those airplanes free from guns
and those terrorists in line.

Now I came up with a plan
I thought would work for sure,
to place in each traveler's hand,
a loaded forty-four.

I felt that this would stack the odds,
and those terrorists would see,
that they should look for other jobs,
and leave us people be.

I asked my wife, what did she think
'bout all those armed people in the sky.
She answered me without a blink,

CARL STONE

and this was her reply. . .

"You'd have wives shootin' husbands.
It would be an awful mess.
It just would cause more problems.
At least that's what I'd guess..."

Now why was that the first thing
that popped into her head?
That there were ladies out there
that would wish their husbands dead?

Now I don't know where that came from
With her it's hard to tell,
and though I look it, I'm not dumb,
now I don't sleep so well!

I guess that I won't mess with it,
leave things the way they've been,
unless the airplane could see fit
to give guns to just the men!

RURAL RAMBLINGS

9-11 INVESTIGATION

A new commission has been formed,
to look into 9-1-1.
Allegations are that we were warned,
and nothin' much was done.

They say we were caught nappin',
that we should'a seen the signs.
But this, before, had never happened,
we'd have to read between the lines.

For who among us could conceive it,
what would transpire on that day?
And if we knew, who would believe it>?
They'd have deemed us crazy anyway.

These Monday mornin' quarterbacks,
after Sunday's game is finally done,
can sit back and look at all the facts,
know how the game could have been won.

This commission should proceed with care,
for what tested us and tried us,
could rise up amidst who might have erred
and finally now divide us.

Both Republicans and Democrats,
died in those towers the same.
Yet some now user their politics,
to find someone to blame.

CARL STONE

The legacy they left that day
was to unify their nation.
It should not be stained in any way
by this investigation.

So, put your politics aside,
for a moment, if you can.
In memory of the ones that died,
and united this great land.

FOREIGN AID

Disaster hit a foreign land.
We send money out of habit.
We dole it out just like sand,
just as if we had it.

Now any friend that can be bought
ain't worth a single dime.
It's a lesson I've been taught
that's true most every time.

A friend that only comes to call
just when he is in need,
really is no friend at all.
Mostly it's just greed.

Where will all these nations be
when we run out of cash?
When there's nothing in our treasury,
they'll be gone real fast.

We should be careful how we spend,
both abroad and here at home,
Cause when it comes down to the end
we'll be standing here alone.

CARL STONE

> WAR, ANY WAR, IS A TERRIBLE, FRIGHTENING THING. THE WAR IN IRAQ WAS BROUGHT INTO MY OWN LIVING ROOM THROUGH THE EXTENSIVE MEDIA COVERAGE ON TV. I WAS STRUCK WITH THE YOUTH OF OUR TROOPS. THEY WERE JUST KIDS, EVEN MANY OF THE JUNIOR OFFICERS. I SUPPOSE THIS HAS BEEN TRUE IN MOST WARS. NOW, WITH THE MAJOR COMBAT OVER, I EXPECT THE TERRORIST WAR WILL GO ON FOR YEARS, I WROTE THIS.

THE IRAQ WAR

Their combat boots struck desert sand
as they stepped down from the plane.
A cry came forth from one young man,
"Where's the one they call Hussein?"

Theirs was such a noble cause,
to set a people free.
And they marched forward, without pause,
in the name of liberty.

They were kids, for the most part,
they'd left home just months before,
but they stood here now, brave of heart,
to face the tests of war.

They came from California,
'crossed to Kansas, up to Maine,
but they'd be the first to warn ya',
they came united 'gainst Hussein.

RURAL RAMBLINGS

Yes, tis true that they were mostly young,
but they'd been educated too.
They'd seen what hate and terror'd done
and they knew what they must do.

Cause ya' don't sit and pet a rabid dog,
just wonderin' when he'll bite.
And ya' don't just lay there like a log,
givin' up without a fight.

The load that was placed in their hands
was more than their backpack,
was the safety of their own homelands
and the freedom of Iraq.

See, they came here not to dominate,
or rule this foreign land.
Their mission was to liberate,
then to lend a helping hand.

Back home protestors lined a street,
No doubt they'd heard about 'em.
They shook their heads and clenched their teeth.
They had enough support without 'em.

Could selfishness have such might
'gainst the people of Baghdad?
That some would not support the fight
for freedoms they already had?

We tried in vain to get support
from Russia, Belgium, France,

CARL STONE

but to make a too long story short,
we grew tired of that dance.

So, as wind whipped sand stung their face
beneath a scorching sun,
they knew not what weapons they would face
before this war was won.

On to Baghdad! Was the battle cry,
and with their allies they pushed on,
with an eagles' courage in their eye
they fought until they'd won.

Those countries laughin' 'hind our back
when we started on that war
watched our troops storm through Iraq
and they don't snicker anymore!

But victory demands a price
that's sometimes hard to pay,
Cause some damn good people lost their lives
in the battles 'long the way.

They say kids aren't what they used to be,
but I would say they are!
Least that bunch that fights for you and me
in a desert way off far.

God bless those kids
and the country they stand for!

IN MEMORIAM

CARL STONE

June 26, 2000

We are here to commemorate the life of a very remarkable woman. Florence Stone. Her life touched everyone here in ways too numerous to mention. In that light I think it's appropriate to briefly highlight the one thing on this earth of which she was most proud, her children. She has, of course, passed the torch on to this next generation. The following are things mom would express today were she able to do so.

Duane, Dullee, you being the oldest, are our leader, our trailblazer. You showed the rest that there is indeed a life after the farm on the hill. You were the first to leave the farm, first to marry, first to give mom a grandchild. Thank you.

Fred, you are our adventurer, our free spirit, you have shown us the strength & elasticity of our roots. No matter how far from home you have traveled, the
instant you let go you were swiftly pulled back home. Thank you for showing us the value of our roots.

Pat, you are our missionary, our evangelist. You have devoted your life to spreading God's word across this country, indeed around the world. You have made your family most proud. Thank you.

Jim, you and I were too stubborn to follow the lead of the first three, we just kept on farmin'. Thanks to you and your family for helping me and mine in the struggle to keep the farm on the hill for the rest of the clan to come home to.

Kath, you, perhaps more than anyone, have been the bonding force that helps hold us together. Your tenacious grasp on family traditions and gatherings has shown us all the value we are to one another, thank you.

Roberta, Bobbie, your upbeat smile, boisterous laughter and entertaining Christmas outfits make each get-together complete. You're also a constant reminder that New Jersey is indeed not a foreign country. Thank you.

Nancy, your role as caregiver for our mom was assumed without hesitation. Thanks for your tireless efforts on our behalf.

Thanks to all of you for the spouses, children and grandchildren you've added to this family. We love them all.

I wrote this poem for you, my brothers and sisters.

FLORENCE STONE

>We're gathered here to honor
>the mom that we all know
>although that woman left us
>quite some time ago.
>
>I'd like to travel back in time
>when I was just a kid
>and think of things she taught us,
>remember things she did.
>
>She taught us to love music,
>A good ole gospel song.
>There's nothin' she loved better
>than to stand and sing along.

"Make a joyful noise unto the Lord,"
she used to say,
"And if you just can't sing a lick,
sing it anyway."

Her sweet soprano voice
had a texture all its own.
Sometimes I heard it in the choir
as if she sang alone.

The EMTs have told me
when Dad took his final ride,
she held his hand and sang to him,
always by his side.

She taught us about family.
She'd be glad that we're all here.
'Cause family love, togetherness,
were things that she held dear.

She taught us to look past our faults,
for those of you that got 'em.
The woman practiced what she preached,
right straight from top to bottom.

She taught us about service
to the ones she loved.
She taught us about service
to the Lord above.

At mealtime all of us were served
before she took her chair
and when we went up to our rooms

clean clothes were always there.

Homemade bread was on the table,
canned goods on the shelf.
She always thought of others first,
never of herself.

She could take a pound of hamburger
and feed the whole darn bunch.
And then she'd take the leftovers
and warm 'em up for lunch.

Now what was left from that meal
she'd scrape out to our ole mutt.
She most never wasted anything,
she just always used it up.

I guess most the stuff she taught us,
if we took a closer look,
came right from the same ole source.
We call it The Good Book.

The Bible was her road map,
it was how she planned her life.
And she could use it as a shield
'gainst any peril, any strife.

I know it must have helped her cope
with the things that you brats did,
'Cause if I can remember right
I was her only perfect kid.

If smiles should mingle with the tears

in this church today,
She loved to hear her children laugh,
she'd a' wanted it that way.

We are our parents' legacy.
We're what they left behind.
And as we travel through our lives,
We best bear that in mind.

The standards that they set for us,
as parents, husbands, wives,
they set not with the spoken word.
They set them with their lives.

So now Ma's sittin' there with Dad,
Clutchin' Mel and Donna to her breast.
They're sittin' there at Jesus's feet,
she's got her final rest.

The heartache that you feel today,
my friends it just won't last.
'Cause as my mom used to say,
"I know this too shall pass."

So this is just so long, Mom,
this is not good-bye.
'Cause we'll all see ya' later
when we meet again on high.

THIS MAN'S LEGACY

January 14, 2018

I cannot sum up this man
with some simple little verse.
For me to even think I can
would just be for the worse.

A man's legacy, some would say,
is a measure of one's worth,
a ruler in some simple way,
of his time here on earth.

The lessons that he taught you kids,
the love he gave his wife,
all the farmin' that he did
throughout his workin' life.

All the smiles he dished out,
all the laughter that he gave,
all the wisdom that he brought
before retiring to his grave.

For us to measure that today
would forever be too tough,
'Cause the only thing I can say –
There's no tape long enough.

CARL STONE

AUNT CAROL

Carol was born a farmer's daughter
back in nineteen seventeen.
On a farm in Tinker Hollow,
youngest child of Lee & Queen.

The things her Mama taught her
on that farm in Tinker Hollow
would serve well the farmer's daughter
in the years that were to follow.

'Cause in nineteen thirty-seven,
a young man stole her heart.
And she felt she was in heaven
when she married good ole Cart.

She had three children she loved dear,
A daughter & two sons.
The girl was perfect, or prett' near,
The boys tried her patience some.

Train up a child in the way he should go,
she read there in The Book
and she set out to make it so.
I'd say she did real good.

But she wasn't one to just stop there,
there were other kids in town.
God's word was written to be shared,
So she spread the word around.

RURAL RAMBLINGS

Kids for Christ and VBS,
she made sure we all had fun,
and I'spose we did our very best
to keep her on the run.

How many Chevys she wore out,
she logged a lotta miles,
haulin' all those kids about,
She logged a million smiles.

Played piano for you and me,
couldn't sing a song without her,
and if we sang a bit off key,
She'd just play a little louder.

She was an ole time farmer's wife,
you'll still find some with some lookin'.
Just pick up a fork and knife
and you'd taste it in her cookin'.

Like, good lard's what makes a pie crust,
That was just a fact,
back in the days 'fore all this fuss
'bout cholesterol and fat.

And the vegetables were sweeter,
if she grew 'em for herself,
'sides that a whole lot cheaper
than off the grocery shelf.

Of course nothing went to waste back then
The Good Lord only knows it.

CARL STONE

If she couldn't put it in a can,
by golly she just froze it.

And if you were to ask her why
she worked the whole day through?
She would have smiled and replied,
"It's just something that you do!"

Her life was helping other people,
Without a second thought
She gathered strength here, 'neath this steeple
every chance she got.

She lived a life full and long
and in that we should rejoice
so today as we sing her song
let us make a joyful noise.

Through all those days, the good and bad,
her faith in God just shone.
In the end it was that faith she had
that carried her on home.

See, her time spent here with you and I
was but one droplet in the sea.
'Cause now she's with Our Lord on high
for all eternity.

WHAT IF?

September 1999

I have no right to speak a word,
I've never known your pain,
but I will speak it anyway,
'cause I've only half a brain.

I know your only human,
and somewhere down the line,
those fateful dreadful words, "What if?",
are bound to cross your mind.

But now I beg you please don't go,
down the "What if" path,
it only leads to sorrow,
loneliness and wrath.

"What if" implies that you were slack,
you could have changed that day,
it tries to make you think, my friends,
you really had a say.

What happened was an accident,
that's plain for all to see,
and nothin's gonna change that.
Not even you or me.

There is but one "What if" path,
that I would let you stray,
and you should guess that this one,

leads a whole new different way.

What if you two had never known,
that pretty blonde-haired kid?
Had never heard the words she spoke,
or seen the things she did?

What if you'd never heard her laugh,
or never seen her dance?
What if she'd never done those things,
had never had that chance?

What if she'd never had you two,
to love her oh so much,
had never known a father's smile,
a mother's loving touch?

She had more joy in her short life,
than many ever know.
And most of it because of you,
don't say that it ain't so.

What if you both grow weary.
As you struggle with you load?
Don't forget you have good friends,
they live just up the road.

RURAL RAMBLINGS

AUNT RUTH

From just Common folk, Ruth was raised,
right in this countryside.
This was where she spent her childhood days
and this is where she died.

She moved out to the great southwest
when she still) had her youth,
and looking back it was the best,
that lifestyle suited Ruth.

I still can see her yet today
in her silver and turquoise.
She wore it in a special way,
with dignity and poise.

She came home to be with those who cared.
We can't imagine what that's worth.
Cause sure enough they were there,
when she passed from this earth.

She lived her long life with honesty
and enjoyed what life would give.
She lived her life with dignity,
and died the way she lived.

When Ruth arrives at heaven's door
the gates will open wide
and a chihuahua pup will bark to her
when she's by Art & Russell's side.

CARL STONE

CARLTON HEAD

Some things been with us for so long
it seems like they'll always be.
Like the early mornin' robin's song
out in the ole pine tree.

Like the clouds that drift across the sky
or the beating of a heart.
Such was the case of one ole guy,
that I called Uncle Cart.

To recount all the time that he spent
in just this simple rhyme,
would be impossible, I fear.
'Spect we'd run out of town.

So I'll talk about some of the stuff
that I remember best.
And though I won't say near enough,
I'll let you fill in the rest.

He made a livin' on the farm
with a top herd of cows.
Most days spent more time in the barn
than he did in the house.

He had hybrid corn and purebred cows
and of both he grew the best.
And as I look back on it now,
he set the bar for all the rest.

RURAL RAMBLINGS

He always kept things up in shape,
and did the best he could,
to do whatever it would take
to keep things lookin' good.

He'd toggle up an old machine
until it'd work again.
When it was runnin' smooth and clean
he'd just stand back and grin.

Yup, he made a livin' on the farm
and he worked hard every day.
But he could also see no harm
in takin' some time out to play.

He flew his own airplane,
up in the sky of blue.
The people that can make that claim
I'd say are precious few.

He played baseball in his youth
and he loved the game since then.
And pound for pound to tell the truth,
the best?? He may have been.

Horseshoes or a game of cards,
he like a good contest.
And if you played 'gainst Uncle Cart,
rest assured you'd get his best.

He hunted woodchucks with Cliff Tyzick,
over hill and over dale.

CARL STONE

And 'fore ole Cliff realized it,
Cart was countin' tails!

He made an Alaskan trip,
mostly 'cause he'd never been.
And after they'd looked round a bit,
they drove back home again.

Still... the most important thing in his life,
after all those things he did,
was his devotion to his wife,
and his own kids and grandkids.

Late years that's all he talked about,
when folks stopped by to talk to him.
And they all left without a doubt
of his undying love for them.

He lived a life full and rich,
did what he had to do,
and left us all with no regrets,
when his time here was through.

Up in heaven there's a baseball game,
one the heavenly saints attend.
And Cart will play, no longer lame,
'cause his legs are young again!

CHARLES TYZICK

The weeks and years that we so treasure,
as we live here on this earth,
will never be the tape to measure
just what our lives were worth.

It's what we did with all those years
that makes our lives worthwhile.
So lest our eyes well up with tears,
let's think of Charles and smile.

Father, husband, brother, son,
He gave each role his best
and I would say when he was done
that he'd passed every test.

For he made this world a better place
For every life he touched.
And put a smile on every face,
Wish we all could give so much.

Charles, filled with goodness, armed with truth
and faithful to the end.
I was proud to share with him my youth,
prouder still to call him friend.

CARL STONE

HAROLD "JACK" JOHNSON JR.

April 9, 2003

It's a shame that a good man's worth
is seldom realized,
until he's gone from this old earth
And we've said our last goodbyes.

Such was the case of one called Jack,
cattle dealin' was his trade,
and he worked with both his brain and back
for every dollar made.

He came into my barn 'fore dawn,
most folks weren't yet awake.
We'd greet each other with a yawn
then some cattle deal we'd make.

I'd joke 'bout how it made no sense,
for me to sell to him,
'cause he's already rich at my expense.
He'd just shake his head and grin.

"I sure would like to give you more,"
I still can hear him say,
"But the wife won't let me in the door
if I lose money again today."

That's mostly what you could expect,
we liked to joke and kid,
but each held a measure of respect

for what the other did.

I s'pose he caught me sleepin' some
and made an extra buck.
But he was as honest as they come
and he had to run the truck.

We'd talk local politics and stuff,
while I just milked along,
until he thought I'd had enough,
then he'd load up and he'd be gone.

His wife and kids were number one,
he made certain of their care.
But he had a passion for his town
that I think today is rare.

Fifty years a fireman,
sixteen years their chief,
sixteen years a councilman,
pursuing his beliefs.

The hours he spent for others good
are too numerous to mention.
He gave to us the best he could
with all honorable intentions.

Yes, he gave much more than he took,
of that I have no doubt.
And if we take a second look
that's what life is all about.

Thanks Jack.

CARL STONE

FATAL CRASH

September 1999

The paper had it written
as another fatal crash.
The people read it sadly,
then tossed it in the trash.

"What a waste of one so young",
they shook their heads and sighed.
If only they could know it,
the newspaper had lied.

One young child, too soon passed on,
was what they had to print.
As to what had really happened,
they never had a hint.

What died there was a family,
What died there was a farm,
What died there was a man and wife,
no longer arm in arm.

What died there was the hopes and dreams
that they once shared together,
everything was whisked away,
as the wind would toss a feather.

They still lived as man and wife
although they were alone.
The building that they lived in

was a house and not a home.

The kids left there in that house
had a mother and a dad,
but they didn't have the parents
they remembered they once had.

They slowly plodded through each day
like robots in a trance.
They barely spoke a single word
although they had the chance.

In the same boat, adrift at sea,
each one would do his best.
One stroked bravely eastward,
the other paddled west.

Sorrow turned to anger,
anger into hate.
They never saw it coming
until it was too late.

The farm was broken into lots
and auctioned just last week.
And when the final gavel fell
neither one could barely speak.

Today she pauses in the door
a tear is in her eye.
She slowly turns and walks away,
never even says good-bye.

This didn't have to happen,

it shouldn't be this way.
There should have been but one lone
death on that fateful day.

Somewhere a paper writes
about another fatal crash.
The people read it sadly
then toss it in the trash.

www.ingramcontent.com/pod-product-compliance
Lightning Source LLC
LaVergne TN
LVHW012247070526
838201LV00090B/141